THE
GIFT
IN **YOUR STORY**

11 Women Share Their
Inspiring Transformational
Journey to Healing

Kelly Snider

Published by Epic Exchanges Media, February 2021
ISBN: 9781777555207

Editor: Danielle Anderson
Proofreader: Lee Robinson - globalconsultant.lee@gmail.com
Typeset: Greg Salisbury
Cover Art: "Transform" by Emily Scott
Cover Design: Tara Eymundson

Dedication

This book is dedicated to the memory of my grandmother, Evelyn Rannard Dingle, the original family storyteller. Sunday evenings would find all generations engrossed in her entertaining tales about her life. She always aspired to share her stories with a wider audience, and that inspired me to provide opportunities for others to do the same.

"Don't die with your music still in you."
Wayne Dyer

Acknowledgements

This book didn't happen overnight—in fact, it's been a dream for several years. The number of people who contributed to keeping this dream alive for me is long, and I will do my best to include everyone.

Thank you to the amazing community of friends, family, and friends-who-have-become-family who encouraged me throughout this journey that started with a small story-sharing conference, became the Epic Exchanges podcast, and then finally saw this book become a reality. You are too numerous to list here, but you know who you are.

To the eleven amazing women who have trusted me through this process and revisited some of the most difficult times in their lives to "reveal the gift" in their challenges: thank you for being vulnerable, for working through the emotions to find another layer of healing, and for having the courage to share your story with someone else who might need your encouragement.

To our partner in publishing, Julie Ann, and to all of Influence Publishing, thank you for walking me (and all of us) through this process and for the incredible learning experience it has been. We wouldn't be here without you.

And to Deborah Sauro: there are no words to show my appreciation. You have been invaluable in making this project a reality and in so many of the ups and downs of this rollercoaster we call life. You are a sounding board, supporter, encourager, and so much more. Thank you, my sister-friend!

Introduction

An epic exchange is any interaction where one or all people come out of it inspired, encouraged, motivated, or even transformed. These moments happen multiple times each and every day, we just have to look for them. They happen even more so when we share our stories—the good times, the challenging times, and yes, even the traumatic and tragic times.

We all have stories that can become an epic exchange for at least one other person; often, it can do this for many. The key is that in the moment, we are usually unable to see the lesson we learned and the impact our story could have. We need to do the work to reveal, heal, and discover the gift in those very difficult times. That's what this book is all about, and what is contained in each chapter that follows: the struggle, the healing process, and now, the sharing of these experiences to help at least one other person who might be going through something similar.

If you have ever struggled with finding your place or purpose in the world or finding meaning in the midst of life's challenges, this book is for you. Find your own inspiration through the stories of these eleven amazing and accomplished women from varied backgrounds as they each share their journey of discovering the gifts of self-love, strength, resilience, forgiveness, belief, healing, and learning more about who they really are.

Our difficult times are not unique, yet the ways in which we come through them and the blessings we discover in that process may be. Often it just takes a little time, perspective, and healing to be able to see the gifts that we received. Or, as Tony Robbins says, "Life doesn't happen TO you, it happens FOR you."

What story do you have to share?

Contents

1

Loving Your Self First

By Emily Scott

"Today, again, I choose myself. My own pride. My own self-respect, my own well-being. I choose not to worry about what they will think. I choose not to worry about disappointing anyone. I choose myself."
Magda Rose

Loving Your Self First

By Emily Scott

I learned of my husband's infidelity two years after it had occurred—two years that were spent with the girl (and her husband and child) in our lives, growing closer, travelling together, sharing dinners, babysitting…all of it. I left my body that day. I still remember looking down at myself in the shower, trying not to fall from the dizzying shock.

There's a reason it's called heartbreak. You can literally feel your chest ripping open, your body tearing in half.

When I met my husband, I truly believed that I was never going to have to worry about having my heart broken ever again. I hadn't been looking for a relationship when we met, or anything close to it. I was getting ready to leave for the Peace Corps, so that's where my head was at. He said he would wait for me; he proposed while I was still overseas to lock it down. He proposed for real once I got home, and I said yes. It was so easy, so relaxed, so natural, so happy. Our friends were annoyed by our cheesiness, the way we talked to each other, how affectionate we were. It really was straight-up bliss and perfection every single day for almost seven years. I could never see him hurting me, which I suppose made it that much more painful, confusing, and traumatic when he did.

When I found out, we were just ending a four-year military assignment overseas and were preparing to return to the States. Our flights were booked. Our dogs' flights were booked. Everything was wound up in such a way that I didn't feel like I could leave even if I wanted to. I was so embarrassed, in shock, and ashamed. I couldn't process anything beyond the moment I was in.

What further twisted the knife is that I had completely released and restructured my career plans to accommodate his, and I struggled and stressed for years to do so. As a military spouse, you essentially sacrifice your career to manage the lifestyle. I was very fortunate to land one of the few decent jobs on the base when we relocated overseas, but I had to take a 55% pay cut in the process despite having a master's degree. The job wasn't in my field, nor was it challenging or inspiring in any way. So, I launched my art practice into a side business and poured myself into it in every spare moment, thinking that building something I could take with me whenever we moved would be the beautiful solution to this stagnation. My mind was constantly consumed by the stress of growing my business into a sustainable source of income and building a satisfying career that would work alongside his military career. And this is what I get in return?

In the days surrounding the confession, Beyoncé blessed us with *Lemonade*, an incredible audio-visual masterpiece birthed from the pain and healing she went through as a result of her husband's infidelity. I convinced myself that my husband and I would make it through this—that it was just a very ugly bump in the road of an otherwise amazing relationship. I mean, if Beyoncé isn't safe from betrayal, none of us are, right?

I spent that first year floating around in a fog of shock, so much so that I don't remember a lot of what happened in that time. I remember getting up at 6:00 a.m. to restore a piece of furniture before it got too hot out, house hunting, cuddling our niece, and crying myself to sleep almost every night, but not much else.

I didn't want to tell anyone what had happened. Aside from the intense shame and embarrassment, no one else is in your relationship. No one knows every word exchanged between the two of you but the two of you. I didn't want anybody else's opinion. I didn't even have the mind space to have conversations with other people about it. I could barely have a conversation with anyone about anything because my thoughts were flooded by something I couldn't even form words about. I felt like if I was going to share anything about it with anyone, I had to share everything. I did tell two mutual friends so they would have an explanation for the abrupt severing of this girl from our lives, and I told them every single detail of the entire situation. It was horrendous; the whole thing would just play over and over in my mind.

One of the main reasons I kept it in was that I knew people were going to make judgments. I didn't want my parents to be mad at my husband or hate him. I didn't want my girlfriends to, you know, want to bury him. I didn't want to have to defend my choice to stay and try to work things out. I was embarrassed, more embarrassed than I've ever been, and so ashamed that I was in this situation. Somehow, I thought that isolating myself with the person who had broken me would help me heal—looking back now, it sounds so ridiculous. But I truly thought we would get past this eventually, and the affair would just fade into the background. "Time heals all wounds," right?

His betrayal didn't fade away, though; it clung onto us, and it changed everything. It tainted every bit of our relationship from the day it happened forward. By him not telling me immediately, he turned one act of betrayal into daily, purposeful betrayals for that entire two-year period I was in the dark being made a fool by both of them.

Over the next four years I slowly rolled through all the phases of grief, sinking into a deep depression that I didn't fully recognize until I began to crawl out of it. Some days I felt okay, some days not. Some days I ended up in the dark place where I cried myself to sleep and didn't know when the pain and sadness would end. But going through that kind of trauma—crawling into the darkest depths of yourself and then having to pull yourself back out—changes you as a person.

At one point during the "dark night of the soul," I went down a YouTube rabbit hole while listening to guided meditations and came across inspirational speaker and educator Esther Hicks, which ended up being a turning point for me. Listening to her workshops helped me understand the basics of the universe again. The better you *feel*, the better it gets; the worse you feel, the worse it gets. And I was never going to feel better about being with my husband after what he did. That heartbreak had taken over my thoughts in an extremely negative way, and I had allowed it to snowball.

It took me almost three years to get to the other side of that tunnel, and once I did, I was no longer the same person. Something had snapped. My resentment, bitterness, and frustration became immense.

Once I transitioned into the anger phase of grief, I was so consumed by it that I had no room for anything or anyone else. And soon, the effects of this on my health became apparent. I began losing excessive amounts of hair, having massive skin reactions to things that didn't previously bother me, and feeling like a weight was sitting on my chest all day. I think the tipping point was waking up after yet another dream about decapitating the girl he had cheated on me with (I have since been reassured by a therapist that homicidal thoughts are normal in such a situation, so long as they stay thoughts). I was so very tired of having these dreams, having her face in my mind, not being able to get through a day without thinking about what they did, being disgusted by it, wanting to tell her what garbage she was, wanting to scream and break things, the list goes on.

The rage led me to finally feeling ready to start talking about what happened. When I told those few mutual friends at the beginning, it felt shameful, painful. Now that I was *choosing* to share my story, telling that first friend felt like an explosion moving away from me. After that, it got easier to share what I'd been going through with a couple of other close friends—ones who were familiar with the situation and the people involved—and that helped as well. The more I was able to talk about it, the further I moved toward the light at the other end of the tunnel, I guess you could say.

Despite forgiving my husband for the mistake itself, the marriage we'd once had was gone. His regret was—and continues to be—deep and relentless, and I know it's real. I also believe he wouldn't make the same mistake twice. But the longer I stayed, the more I felt like I was living with the ghost of my previous self. The betrayal was so deep, so cruel, so layered that it had done irreparable damage to our relationship. Perhaps if he had told me that night, the next day, the day after that... then maybe we could have purged her from our lives and moved past it. But he let me spend two years getting closer and closer to her, the both of them carrying on around me like nothing had happened.

Those two years are what broke me. The woman who joyously chose to be his wife, who changed her name for his birthday, she's the one who crawled inside herself and died. The woman who emerged is someone else.

One day, during a week of work training in which I hadn't been able to focus on or retain most of what was said, I had a colossal panic attack spurred by the frustration that this was still filling my brain and getting in the way of my goals. When I told him later, the conversation devolved into a sobbing, can't-breathe breakdown about how I was *still* so sad so often. I told him I needed to go away for a while and figure things out. I had gotten so low, so dark, that I stopped caring about anything else except doing whatever I could to bring myself back to happiness. He told me he understood if I still wanted to leave after all this time—that he was the one who screwed up. A slight weight lifted upon hearing that.

Throughout all of this, my physical and mental health were noticeably suffering. Eventually, two of my closest girlfriends put their collective feet down and demanded that I remove myself from the situation to at least make a decision. They called out my intense self-isolation and worse-than-normal workaholism. They told me that I was a very hot mess, and that it was time to take care of myself. Having brutally honest friends is very important, and I am so grateful for mine.

I also found an excellent therapist (four years later than I should have), and one day she called me out on betraying myself. That one was a gut punch. I had known for a long time that our relationship was permanently broken and that I needed to leave, but I was hesitating because I didn't want to hurt him. I was still putting his feelings above my own. I had to acknowledge that I wasn't okay. I had to take care of myself, I had to choose myself, and I had to love myself more than I loved him.

Finally, after four years of trying to "recover" from my husband's mistake, I realized that it wasn't my job to work it out. It wasn't my job to figure out how to get through it, how to get past it, how to make it work, how to save our marriage. This wasn't my fault, nor was it my problem to fix. Sometimes things are so broken that they simply can't be put back together. I had lost myself in both the love and the pain of our relationship. I had to focus on my own happiness and well-being, and I had to carry on creating my life—even if it didn't turn out the way we'd planned.

I really try to live with no regrets. Even when something terrible happens or things don't go the way I expect them to, there's always knowledge to be gleaned, a lesson to be learned, or wisdom to be gained. I think the only regret I have from this entire situation is not listening to my gut. When this girl first crossed our paths she had more red flags than Disneyland, yet I chose to ignore them. Her lifestyle choices weren't any of my business until they were, I guess. I also had a weird feeling on the night of the betrayal, but at the time I truly wasn't worried. I trusted my husband and didn't think he would ever, ever do anything like that. We were committed. We were married. Our love was amazing. But my intuition was right, and I'll never question it again.

Once I made the decision to leave and knew that it was the right step to take, the weight began to lift. I loved him, and still do, but those feelings have morphed into that of close friends and family. I didn't want any more pain, and I understood that

I had to be the one to remove myself from the situation or the pain would never end.

New Mexico had been calling me for years, and I soon found myself on a hillside outside of Santa Fe with a shamanic practitioner—a wonderful coincidence provided by the universe. The ground was sprinkled with quartz crystals, and I was surrounded by a beautiful mixture of blazing gold aspens and fluffy evergreens. I stayed for a month, but by the end of the first week I knew that I couldn't go backwards from there. It wasn't that I hated my husband, or even disliked him. I loved him—I wouldn't have tried so hard for so long if I didn't—but I could no longer be his. I could no longer feel obligated to him or gift him with my last name.

By the time I left New Mexico, I was clear and resolute—I hadn't felt like that in years. And the further I came into clarity, the more I realized I had been in that dark fog for so, so long. But had I not gone there, I wouldn't be here, and I am beyond excited to see what's ahead.

When I was throwing up from crying so hard those first few weeks, I never imagined I would be sharing this with anyone, let alone to you, beautiful stranger, in actual print. But as I was healing and coming through this pain, I knew I wasn't alone—this sort of thing happens all the time, unfortunately, especially in the military. This experience gave me a new understanding of the laws of the universe and how our thoughts create the world around us, and I want women and girls in particular to understand how powerful you are, and how completely the universe supports you. I want you to know that you're not alone.

You CAN start over at any moment. You can deconstruct and rebuild at any point in your life, even if you had never planned to start over again. You are not starting from scratch, but from experience. You can reCREATE your life exactly as you desire. You're capable of being, doing, and having literally anything you can imagine for yourself—the universe wouldn't put those thoughts there otherwise. You CAN trust yourself to create your life, and it can be more beautiful than anything you've experienced thus far. How exciting is that? Every day is an opportunity to forge a beautiful new path.

Truly loving and committing to your Self is the foundation of this. I'm not speaking of selfishness, self-absorption, narcissism, vanity, all those words that you aren't. I'm talking about putting your oxygen mask on first. I'm talking about recognizing your needs and taking action to meet them. I'm talking about prioritizing your mental and physical health so that you can love your loved ones from the best and healthiest version of yourself. I'm talking about making sure your vase is full and stable FIRST, and that you're not empty from trying to water everyone else. I'm talking about *listening* to your Self.

Your Self is sacred and so much more powerful than we've been led to believe. Patriarchal ideals have told us that women are untrustworthy, and what has this belief led us to do? To question our own intuition. To listen to others' opinions above our own, including what we believe they *might* say or think. Why do we do that? Who could possibly know what is best for you more than your actual higher Self?

Our higher selves are part of our collective Source (or whatever you choose to call her), and that's what we're all trying to hear. Your intuition/self/gut/knowing is a direct line of communication to Source. Once you line up with that, the world is your cupcake. Your thoughts are placing vibe-based orders with your higher Self/Source/the Universe, which means you can cook up anything you can imagine. Anything. Everything is possible, and your potential is limitless.

Despite the horrendous pain of these past few years, I'm

so grateful. I'm grateful for the love my husband and I shared while we had it. I'm grateful for the beauty we experienced. I'm grateful for his family, which will always be my family despite our relationship changing seasons. I'm grateful that we were able to end our marriage on respectful, accepting, loving grounds, and that we continue to be close friends. Most of all, I'm grateful for this journey through the highest highs and the lowest lows. Without such extremes, I never would have experienced such epic love, joy, and romance, and I never would have been led back to myself.

When you find yourself in pain, use that pain to make art, physically and metaphorically. Use it to dig into the deepest caves within yourself and find the diamonds. Use it to level up into the next version of yourself. Use it to create your life as you dream it. Life is so beautiful, and you are so much more powerful than you think. Literally anything is possible; you just have to choose your Self.

About Emily Scott

Emily Scott is a project manager and Salesforce enthusiast by day and an award-winning self-taught artist by night. Born and raised in the Kootenai Valley in northwest Montana, she headed to Seattle for college and grad school before spending several years overseas interning, participating in Peace Corps, travelling, eating, and seeking epic nature, all the while growing her art business. Nineteen countries later, she is back in the Pacific Northwest making art inspired by the natural wonders from her travels and surroundings, creating works that emanate the constant soothing-yet-powerful energy of our universe.

Emily is passionate about empowering women to step into their true Selves, to love themselves, and to take control of their own personal uprising, whatever that may look like.

www.emilyscottartist.com
Instagram: @emilyscottartist

2

Becoming a Bonus Mom

By Deborah Sauro

"We must take care of our families wherever we find them."
Elizabeth Gilbert

Becoming a Bonus Mom

By Deborah Sauro

My journey to motherhood did not follow the traditional path. After going through three failed rounds of IVF, I didn't think it would ever happen. I was almost forty years old with high blood pressure caused by the drugs associated with the fertility treatments, so I was told that even adoption was a long shot. However, once I got over the disappointment, sadness, and grief of not being able to conceive, I realized my husband and I were already a family of two, and we had the ability to take in others who might need some unconditional love and support. And so, we did just that.

In truth, though, I have been "adopting" people my whole life. For much of my childhood, we had a variety of people living with us—my family never let anyone who needed a home be without. There were people who needed a place to call home for a short while and kids whose parents were trying to work through challenging times. It was natural for my brother and I to share our parents with lots of other folks, and my mother always said that there was room in our hearts for everyone.

The first time I "adopted" someone was in elementary school. There was a young girl in my class whose home life was not easy, and for whom school was difficult. I never wanted her to feel unimportant or unappreciated, so I started making small mistakes in my class work so that she wouldn't be alone in her confusion. This went on for some time until my mother finally sat me down and explained that this was not the way to help her—that rather than denying my abilities, I should share my knowledge, encourage her, and support her through the challenges she was facing.

The next person was a young girl whom I started to babysit when I was eleven years old and she was three. Her dad was a single parent and starting a new career in media, so he had odd working hours that often ran late into the night. My entire family adopted this sweet girl and her dad, and we became their surrogate family. There were evenings when we would leave our front door unlocked so that she could be dropped off for the night. We would wake up, get her dressed, take her to school, and pick her up at the end of the day. She became my little sister. There were times when I was a bit jealous of the attention she received from my mom—I was becoming a self-conscious, insecure teenager—but again my mom explained that her heart could expand to love all of us the same. This was a great lesson in the capacity for love we all possess.

In my early twenties, I began volunteering for an organization that worked with high school kids. We met weekly with these kids, took them to camp, counselled them, and supported them. It was through this group that I met a girl who was in foster care and lived just down the road from me. She had a lot of anger issues and would lash out at her foster parents, and eventually they felt they could no longer care for her. She was moved into a group home several kilometres away, forcing her to give up her group of friends and her foster family, whom she truly did love. I spent a lot of time with her and tried my best to support her as she grieved. When she had to go to court to determine where she would be placed next, I went to the courthouse to be with her during her hearing. I wasn't able to be in the courtroom itself, but at least she knew someone was there for her. Unfortunately she grew away from me over time, but I know that I supported her as best as I was able to.

As I got older, I stopped adopting others as often and eventually forgot all about it. By the time I'd reached my mid-twenties, I'd had some unsuccessful relationships and began to feel that I would never get married. I was fine with that. However, I always imagined myself with kids—I dreamed about the children I would have, but never about the husband.

When I was in my late twenties, I decided to get out of my rut and take a job working in the gift shops of a cruise ship. My dream of having kids of my own was slowing ebbing away, but I still found myself being the mother hen to the younger shop staff. I was blessed to comfort and support an incredible young man as he wrestled with telling his family he was gay. I quietly held him while he cried on my shoulder, fearing that his mom would reject him. All I could do was reassure him that his mom would never stop loving him. Eventually he did tell his family, who thankfully embraced him and showed him nothing but love and support.

I still didn't imagine myself ever getting married, but then I met the man who changed my mind. Tony and I spent one and a half years sailing the Caribbean while working on board before deciding that we would disembark and start our life together on dry land. We headed off to Italy, where he was from, and moved in with his family in a very small community. We then started looking for a business that we could work in together, although this was complicated by the fact that I didn't speak much Italian. After six months of searching with no work to be found, I was feeling a little overwhelmed. We decided I should head home for Christmas and we would make a decision about our future in the New Year.

In January, Tony came to stay with my family and me. After some discussion, we decided that we would get married and make Canada our home as it would be easier for both of us to find employment here. That April we had a small family ceremony on the sundeck of the home I had grown up in and settled into our life together.

We lived with my parents for four years while we saved enough money to buy our first home. Once we were in our own space, we started to think about having a family. We didn't exactly make a point of trying to get pregnant, but if it happened, it would be a blessing. After several years with no success, we went to see my doctor and discovered that I had fluid-filled cysts on my fallopian tubes. I underwent surgery to remove them, which we thought would resolve the problem. It didn't. After another year, we went back and found out that the cysts had regrown, and that this time the only option was to remove the fallopian tubes entirely. This meant that I would not be able to get pregnant without medical intervention—something that was so difficult to hear after I had been so sure I would have kids.

We decided to investigate the possibility of IVF, and the doctor we met with felt we were good candidates. Due to the high cost of the procedure, we decided we could try one time, and only one. We did all the preliminary tests, got the medications, and started the two weeks of hormone shots that had to be taken twice daily. As a person who suffered through allergy shots as a child and who to this day does not enjoy needles, the thought of injecting myself was too much. So, Tony bravely took on this task. As I needed the shots twice a day, I would have to go down to the restaurant where he worked so he could give me the injection in his office. I absolutely hated the shots and would end up in tears every time. The crazy things you do to have a baby!

The day came when we were ready for the egg retrieval, and it went well—apparently, I can produce a lot of eggs. But when we returned to the office two days later, we were told that only three had fertilized and could be implanted. We stayed positive as three chances were better than none, and I was happy to rest and recline for a couple of days while we hoped for the best. Sadly, after anxiously waiting to be able to take the pregnancy test, it turned out negative. Heartbroken, we figured we were just not meant to be parents. But as Tony told me constantly, we were already our own little family of two.

A few months later, I was checking my bank statement and discovered that some money had been deposited into our account—enough to cover another round of IVF. I could not find out who had done it; my mom always said it was my guardian angel. Eventually I discovered it was my brother who had given us the money as he very much wanted our dream of having a child to come true. So, we tried again. Another two weeks of shots, lots of tears, and only two fertilized eggs that did not result in a pregnancy. We'd had the implantation done on September 10, 2001, and the doctor believed that stress of what came next had had a negative effect on my body. He felt that we should give it another try if we could—that we still had a chance at successfully conceiving.

We began investigating the idea of adopting, but I was advised that due to my age and health issues we were not likely candidates. Another heartbreak. My brother once again secretly deposited money into our bank account for one last IVF attempt, and this final hope was crushed when I found out I was not pregnant on Mother's Day, while on a Mother/Daughter retreat with my own mom. I was devasted. Again, my husband reminded me that we were already a family, and that we were blessed to be able to be there for other people who might need us.

Throughout this time, I was working as an operations/inventory manager for a home furnishing company. I oversaw a team of young men who worked in our stockroom, and I suddenly found myself becoming a den mother to them. I made sure they got to work on time, had lunch, and were able to have time off for their studies. After several years the company opened an off-site warehouse and transferred me there to manage the space, so my boys and I headed off to set up and operate the warehouse together. This is where we became a tight-knit family. We developed a close bond, and I found myself making sure they were all taken care of. I bought food for lunches so they had a least one solid meal a day and treats for days when stock transfers kept us busy. We had Easter egg hunts, Thanksgiving lunches, and Christmas tree decorating parties. Every Christmas eve, we took time to be together and open the presents we had brought for each other. We celebrated first loves and graduations, grieved through losses, and supported and loved each other unconditionally. Their own mothers accepted me as their "other mom," and it meant the world to me to that they appreciated the relationship I had with their boys.

I had an especially close relationship with one of the young men, and he was a huge support for me when my mom passed away from cancer—our roles reversed for a time while he helped me heal from that loss. He was also with me when I got the call that my father had had a heart attack and things didn't look good. As I was frantic and scared, he comforted me, called our store manager, explained what was happening, got everything closed up at the warehouse, and arranged for me to go to the hospital to be with my dad. My father didn't make it, and I will be forever grateful that this young man was there to support me once again.

We all moved on to new schools and careers over time, but our relationships have remained close. I was blessed to have recently been invited to the wedding of one of these men, and I was happy to discover that one of my other "sons" was a groomsman. We had an amazing reunion, and I was grateful that our bond had not changed. I was still their "other mom."

When I started working in the restaurant owned by my husband and brother, I once again found myself looking out for our young staff. We encouraged, coached, and supported a great group who became my new kids. I was fortunate to be able to support one young lady through a lot of personal situations. The more we worked together, the closer we became and the more people believed she was my own daughter. I was honoured when people said this—while she may not have been related by blood, she was my daughter in my heart. We remain close to this day, and I have watched as she has grown into an amazing young woman and become a mother to her own little girl.

After a couple of years of working very long hours for weeks on end, my husband and I decided that we needed to find a better work-life balance and chose to leave the restaurant. We continued to remain in close contact with our staff, though, and one day we found out that a young lady from Italy was in need of a place to live. Without any hesitation, we invited her to stay in our home. She moved into the little suite in our basement that had been home to so many people and became part of our family. She came to us for advice and guidance, and we tried to be there for her as I know her own parents would have been. When she got sick with a serious cold/flu that fall, we moved her upstairs to our spare bedroom so that we could look after her.

In the summer of 2017, we decided that the cost of maintaining a hundred-year-old house—which had been in my family for over sixty years—had become too much to manage and was holding us back from realizing our dream of spending half our time in Italy with our Italian family. So, we chose to sell the house. But before we left, we wanted to have one last big family Christmas dinner. This had been my mother's favourite holiday, and she always included lots of family and friends who were in need of somewhere to celebrate. Our dinner table was always full of love and laughter, and I wanted to honour that one last time. We invited family and a very special group of friends, including our Italian daughter and her best friend who had never really celebrated Christmas here in Canada. We also invited the manager of our restaurant and her partner, my aunt, my cousin, and my dear friend who had just lost her father to cancer and whose family were going to celebrate elsewhere. We made sure that we had small presents under the tree for everyone and cooked an amazing Italian-themed dinner. The joy that I felt while watching this group of people who meant so much to me laughing and celebrating together was the perfect way to honour the legacy of my parents and the home they created. I also realized that I didn't just "adopt" young people, but also people who needed somewhere to call home and someone to love them unconditionally.

While I was not physically able to have children of my own, I now know in my heart that I have always been a mom—a bonus mom to those that have needed one—and for that I am truly blessed.

About Deborah Sauro

Deborah was born and raised in a home that welcomed anyone and everyone. She and her husband have continued this tradition throughout their marriage, taking in anyone who needs a place to stay and a family to love them. She has been inspired to continue the legacy left by her parents to embrace those around her who need unconditional love, understanding, and support.

Deborah spent thirty-five years working in various retail and hospitality positions, including two years spent working aboard a cruise ship in the Caribbean where she met her husband. She also worked as a makeup artist in film and television. Since semi-retiring in 2018, she has worked as an assistant with an events management company and is currently creating social media posts for a friend's company.

While currently living in Squamish, BC, Deborah is lucky enough to have family all over the world and enjoys splitting her time between her two homes, one in Canada and one in Italy.

3

The Feather

By Terry Fodë

"An effort made for the happiness of others lifts us above ourselves."
Lydia Maria Francis Child

The Feather

By Terry Fodë

My husband and I live in Northwestern Ontario. It is a huge expanse of land and lakes which is the traditional territory of eighty-eight First Nations, twenty-five of which are only accessible by air or by ice roads in the winter. Due to the lack of resources for secondary and tertiary education, many First Nation youth must make the difficult decision to leave their home on reserve and fly to the city to continue their education. This happens right at an age when they are trying to determine and solidify their identities and sense of self—right when they need their families and community support most.

Already there has been a crisis of suicide among Indigenous youth on reserve. Historical and intergenerational trauma; community distress due to poor living conditions; a lack of food security, clean water, and health services; and a fragile state of mental wellness are some of the factors that contribute to this heartbreaking situation. When the decision is made to leave their homes and head to a city, I can only assume they feel both terrified and exhilarated. However, moving away brings its own set of issues. Being away from family, experiencing loneliness, feeling a loss of identity, fearing discrimination and racism—all these factors increase the chance that these young people will suffer from depression and anxiety. This may then lead them to get involved with substance abuse or, even worse, to end their own lives.

While I am not Indigenous myself, I went through my own phase of despair and depression in my youth. As I enter mid-life, I have now turned inward to find meaning in my journey here on Earth. How can I make a difference while I am here, and what legacy can I leave behind? I sought the guidance of a personal coach to help me focus my ideas, and I concluded that I could take my love of growing food and use it to help teach others to do the same—particularly those in remote areas who are without food security.

As I set out on this mission, I was introduced to Nomad, an Ojibwa man who was driven to find a way to occupy the youth in his community with productive activities. In particular, he wanted to get them involved in a community garden and greenhouse. He desired to teach them skills, both traditional and modern, that would make them self-sufficient and give them and their community hope for the future. As I have gotten to know him, I have learned more about what life on reserve is truly like and the challenges Indigenous youth face while living there—the lack of motivation, loss of hope, and fear of leaving to go to school. He himself has children who are struggling to navigate these very issues.

Sadly, only a few weeks after we first met to discuss our

ideas for the community garden, Nomad's seventeen-year-old son—who was away from home for schooling—passed away in what was ruled a suicide. Ten months later his niece also died unexpectedly, and then another niece a month after that. These heartbreaking events are just one family's tragedy, but they reflect the reality for many families both on reserve and off. According to Statistics Canada, First Nations people die by suicide at three times the rate of non-Indigenous Canadians, with the highest rates being seen in youth and young adults. The Chief Coroner of Ontario attributes this to the erosion of mental health in these individuals—to an insidious hopelessness that develops at a young age.

These startling numbers, along with Nomad's losses, motivated me to find a solution to bring hope to these youth who are struggling in the same way I once did.

Anxiety is a natural reaction to stress, and all teens will experience stress in their daily lives. However, ongoing anxiety can lead to depression, and both of these conditions, if left untreated, will only become more intense and isolating. Therefore, it is important not only for youth but also for the adults in these youths' lives to watch for signs of these conditions: emotional changes, social changes, physical changes, sleep disturbances, poor school performance, panic attacks, and destructive behaviours. All of these interfere with relationships and daily functions, and the youth are often torn between wanting to belong and a fear of rejection—between wanting to succeed and a fear of failure. And don't forget the inevitable hormonal surges which, when paired with a lack of skills to deal with all the new feelings that accompany them, can be overwhelmingly challenging to navigate. I know this all from personal experience.

The first day of school is never easy, at least not for someone who is generally introverted and struggles with being in large groups, but the first day of Grade Nine was particularly difficult for me. I had cut my hair short over the summer—hair that had been down nearly to my waist—and I almost immediately did not like it. As a result, I was feeling very self-conscious about my looks and was uncomfortable with the attention my new hairstyle was bringing me. Add to that the shuffling between homeroom and other classes, searching for friendly faces in the crowds, meeting new teachers, and having to speak up to acknowledge attendance, I was overwhelmed by what I now know was anxiety. Teachers who had taught me the previous year knew I went by "Terry"—derived from my middle name, "Teresa"—and they corrected their roster accordingly. However, those who did not know me from any other wallflower called out my legal name, "Helen." I did not have the confidence to tell them what I preferred to be called as the anxiety I was experiencing melted away any self-assurance I previously possessed. The other students began to snicker and stare, which only made me more aware of my weirdness. I wanted to shrink into myself and disappear.

My acquiescence to being called my legal name raised a lot of questions from my friends, but I didn't really have an answer for any of them. I couldn't explain how I was feeling. I think I made something up about purposely changing my name and even tried to convince myself that it was true. After all, I truly DID want to be someone else, anyone else, although I hadn't planned on switching my name.

Thus began the school year, one that would turn into months of struggling to make sense of my emotions, figure out my life, find direction and meaning, and navigate all the typical challenges that are thrown at a teenager when their hormones change.

Throughout my adolescence, I frequently felt alone and misunderstood. My thoughts were constantly in turmoil, and I often felt angry, sad, and frustrated all at the same time without really understanding why. I felt that I had no one to talk to about this, so I started keeping a diary in earnest when I was eleven and continued writing in it into my teens. Journaling was a way for me to get out the emotions and ideas that were swirling around inside me. I could release things by writing them down, and rereading entries helped me to work through my thoughts or calm myself down. However, this could also backfire as I would fixate on issues and overanalyze my thoughts into the wee hours.

You may wonder why I didn't turn to my family for support; in truth, I didn't feel like it was an option. I was the only girl of four children, and my brothers did not understand the drama of a teenaged girl's life—the physical and hormonal changes, the emotional rollercoaster of crushes, the fluctuating friendships—and were experiencing their own struggles. My parents were not really available, physically or emotionally. Both worked full-time jobs and were busy, distracted by their responsibilities. They had a low tolerance for my "moodiness." I realize now that they were dealing with their own insecurities and issues—that they had their own lives going on with financial and relationship pressures. However, at this critical time in life, I perceived I wasn't loved and felt quite disconnected from my family. I would often shut myself away in my room to lose myself in books or crafts. I would also escape to friends' houses or to babysitting jobs where I could pretend to be a part of their seemingly normal lives or dream of my own future family, at least for a short time.

Despite how isolated I felt, I wasn't completely alone. I had made a small group of friends in elementary school who stuck with me through high school and whom I am still honoured to call friends today. We participated in church, Girl Guides, drama, and choir. Through those experiences, we strengthened our bonds enough that if I did end up lashing out when my head was not in the right space, they were gracious enough to forgive me and move on. Some of their families were surrogate families for me, and they helped me to survive my teens and keep me on the straight and narrow—away from alcohol, drugs, and bad behaviour.

As I began to explore how I could help the Indigenous communities of Northern Ontario, I reflected on what I learned through my own experiences. How did I manage to survive and find hope as a teenager? How did I drag myself out of despair and darkness to manage my depression and anxiety? What would have made it easier for me? When I look back at my high school years and how I navigated the challenges, I saw that I purged my emotions onto paper or leaned on my friends (although it is advisable to have adults to talk to as well). I also engaged in meaningful activities and supportive groups—places where I had safe friendships, common goals to complete community projects, and good role models. It was in these groups that I learned one of the best lessons I have learned in life: when I am feeling down and hopeless, I always feel better when I refocus my thoughts on helping others. This allows me to gain perspective on my own situation and lift my spirits by bringing a smile to someone else's face.

Considering that the Indigenous youth who have left home to pursue education are already lacking their usual support networks, it is imperative to make these activities and groups available to them. They need comfortable spaces where they can meet others with common goals, make safe friendships, and speak openly about what they are going through and what they may need to help them cope. They need places where adults can look out for the telltale signs of depression and anxiety and reach out to find out what might be going on in their lives. We need to promote the development of key skills to help these youth become resilient and be able to navigate the inevitable stressors they will encounter, such as the ability to develop positive self-talk and self-compassion; to embrace assertiveness and self-confidence; to understand the importance of effort over outcome; to accept failure, struggles, and challenges as learning opportunities; to engage with diverse people by talking and listening; and to explore new ideas and not limit one's horizon. This is also important for the youth who remain at home who may feel alienated from their usual support networks for whatever reason.

When teens and young adults have the opportunity to join a group that works toward a common goal, it not only helps them to build relationships and skills but also gets their minds off their own stresses and puts their focus on others. In so doing, they will begin to feel good about themselves, find a sense of purpose, have goals, and gain some perspective on their own situations. The lesson that lifting and loving others helps me to lift and love myself became the base from which I launched my ideas to help the Indigenous youth.

With this philosophy in mind, I have become involved in two projects. First, I am supporting Nomad in his efforts to develop a community garden and greenhouse as well as a building for the youth club that is currently based out of his home. This will create a safe space with wholesome activities, no drugs or alcohol, food for those who need it, supportive adults who do not judge, and the opportunity to learn gardening and other skills. The youth will help to plant the garden, build the greenhouse, grow the foods, and sell produce within the community to assist with providing an affordable food supply. Food security is a challenge in these remote areas, so helping bring healthy, fresh food to their community will hopefully give these youth a sense of purpose and pride.

Secondly, I support a non-profit organization in Thunder Bay which combines youth development with urban agriculture. It is a safe place for young people from all walks of life to develop gardening and food preparation skills while also learning how food plays a crucial role in health, resilience, and the independence of individuals and communities alike. It is an opportunity for them to engage with their community and build strong connections, which in turn grows their self-confidence and fosters healthy life choices. Some of the benefits these youth have received include improved communication skills, the ability to work and make connections with others, and the opportunity to gain transferable skills and grow their résumé. It is a safe, non-judgemental place to overcome their barriers and challenges.

The importance of both this program in the city and the opportunity on reserve are immeasurable. When the youth involved in these projects see that what they are doing is helping others, they can begin to believe that change is possible and that there is hope for the future.

Depression and anxiety are difficult no matter what age one experiences them, but it is particularly challenging for teenagers. Having gone through debilitating bouts of depression and anxiety throughout my adolescence and into adulthood, I have built a resilient spirit and an empathy for others going through similar struggles. In a search to lift and love myself, I have learned that lifting and loving others is powerful medicine.

It is important to choose to see the positive in our

experiences and use our voices to bring awareness to those who may not yet recognize it themselves. In particular, I want to call attention to the great need for support among the youth of our First Nations communities.

As I walked along the river near my home the other day, I came upon an eagle feather lying among the rocks. Knowing that eagle feathers are significant to the First Nations people, I asked Nomad the meaning of this feather. He excitedly responded that it is a gift—that the eagle had given it to me because I have been attempting to connect with his people. Another friend from the West Coast agreed and told me that feathers are gifts from the Ancient Ones, meant to come to us when we need the love and comfort of the Creator. When we receive one, it is recognition that we are doing good work. It is also medicine for our hurts, and once we are restored, those healing powers should be paid forward. The feather is a sign that it is time for me to use my voice to advocate for others and to share important messages that need to be heard.

I am honoured to have received this gift, especially at a time when not only do I need the love and comfort of the Creator, but so many others do as well. It is my hope that the medicine I am receiving through my efforts to help others will be paid forward to the Indigenous youth and their communities.

About Terry Fodë

Terry Fodë is known for wearing a lot of hats. Some of her past employment includes working on cruise ships internationally, marketing vacation ownership properties while living in Mexico, and providing project support and coordination for the construction and commissioning of a cyclotron facility. She currently works as quality assurance and a lab technician in radiopharmacy.

When not working, Terry can be found with her hands in the dirt or out enjoying nature. Passionate about self-reliance, she grows her own vegetables and practices food storage. She is currently pursuing projects that combine helping remote communities increase their food security with helping youth from these communities gain a passion for self-reliance.

Originally from British Columbia, Terry has called Northwestern Ontario home for the past thirteen years. Her love of languages, art, and culture has recently led her to explore the history, artwork, food and culture of indigenous communities in her area.

Email: terry.fode@hotmail.com

4

Love Found Me

By Kristin Ormiston

"If your heart is broken, make art with the pieces."
Shane Koyczan

Love Found Me

By Kristin Ormiston

When 2010 arrived, I was forty-one years old and two decades into a difficult marriage. I had married for love, but it had never been an easy union—we both had our issues and were caught in a cycle of dysfunction. And as I looked toward the future, I realized I had a decision to make about what I wanted those years to look like.

Despite ending up in these rocky times, my husband and I had a fairy-tale beginning. I had been living in a stone castle on the English countryside and attending a college nearby when a Canadian cohort received some tragic news. Her close friend had been killed in a car accident at the age of twenty-two, leaving behind a husband and two babies just twenty-two months and eight months old. I sent a letter of condolences to Stephen, this twenty-one-year-old widower in the prairies whom I had never met, because I felt a connection to him. I had also recently suffered a tragic loss; my childhood friend had died of leukemia the year before, a few short weeks after I attended his high school graduation as his date.

In response to my note of condolence, Stephen wrote me back and then phoned me at the college. So began our cross-continental romance. Seven months later, I returned from Europe to Canada and met Stephen in person. On December 2, 1989—ten months after beginning our correspondence—we got married and I adopted my husband's two toddlers as my own. Over the next few years Stephen and I had another two children, leaving our hands more than full. We were now in our mid-twenties with four children ages six and under.

Our marriage did okay for some years. We loved each other and our children a great deal. We both worked in the performing arts for most of our married life, enjoying some wonderful successes in performing live theatre across Western Canada. It was our shared joy to bring music, laughter, and tears to audiences near and far. But within our marriage, we had a lot working against us.

Along with my husband's history of early childhood trauma, I had my own shortcomings. Like so many others who struggle with personal issues, I had been raised within a dysfunctional family system. My father had no ill intentions, but he had a personality disorder that made him incapable of making deep emotional connections or being aware of the emotional needs of his family members. He was a charismatic and popular man who thrived on gleaning attention from others, and as a gifted and personable child I was excellent at assisting my father in acquiring the attention he craved. This role was the foundation of our relationship, and while it was a warm exchange, it was not healthy for my development. Throwing my energies into doing this for him meant that I missed out on attending to my own interests and personal growth—the very things that would have enabled me to establish myself as an emotionally healthy and independent adult. The development of my personality had an overemphasis on interpreting and meeting the emotional and physical needs of others. In contrast, I was underdeveloped in the area of discerning my own needs, goals, or desires. This prevented me from becoming a properly independent adult, which brought with it a lot of shame and confusion.

Between my inadequacies, my husband's history of trauma, and the fact that we were raising four children at such a young age, we were always under a lot of stress and often in counselling. Nothing seemed to work. By 2010, I had become so lonely within my marriage that I was becoming attracted to other men. This terrified me. I feared I would betray my family by entering into an extramarital affair, and I was not willing to risk hurting my children in that way. I acknowledged that this attraction was a symptom of my loneliness and unhappiness, and I realized it was time for me to face my inability to solve our problems.

After many years of frustration and sadness, and after working with several therapists in an attempt to fix things, I decided that continuing to live in a dysfunctional marriage was not the best use of my time on this planet. So, I finally asked Stephen for a divorce. It was the most difficult and painful decision of my life. I felt no ill will toward my husband, and it devastated me to hurt him and my family by dissolving the marriage. But in the end, I knew this was what I needed to do in order to have integrity toward myself.

The first year after the split felt like a car accident. My family was angry at me for ruining something that seemed to be working for everybody except me, although I knew it wasn't really working for them either. My never-ending tolerance for the dysfunction within our family had been perpetuating their own unhealthy behaviours. These were hard days; I was in my own extreme grief in the midst of a room full of anger toward me. But I managed to live in these days, and I felt everything within those moments. I believe that being fully present for every emotion, including deep pain, is the only way to access the fullness of life. It is my experience that when there is great sorrow, we can use the energy of our grief to dig a deeper well which can hold more joy in the days that are yet to come. I also believe that if we fully focus on our present circumstances during these times of sorrow, we are better able to unravel the mystery of what our next project and experience should be.

For me, the next project was a great big change. Now that I was going through this time of domestic upheaval, I reassessed my job opportunities. My lifelong passion has always been the education of young children, but pursuing this dream in Canada would require agreeing to a vocational life where I felt I would not be valued, respected, or remunerated the way I deserved. For that reason, I turned my eyes toward Japan. I knew that Japanese society greatly valued education and children of all ages, so I felt this was a better place to follow this passion. I was able to secure a job that I was led to believe involved working at a preschool in Tokyo, and my employer arranged for my working visa. My departure was six months after the 2011 earthquake, so thousands of foreigners had fled Japan; this opened the doors of opportunity for me, including the rare offering of a three-year visa.

At this time, my four children were barely adults, with my youngest son about to turn eighteen. It may have seemed odd for me to leave them like this, but I believed that if I stayed with my family and continued in my role of outcast and failure,

I would be of little use to my children because they would continue to believe the stories being told about me. Friends and family wanted me to work as a cashier at the local grocery store or be a manager of an apartment strata, but I felt that these occupations were not how I wanted to spend my precious time. I wanted to invest my time and gifts into the lives of children in ways that were not available to me in Canada, and I wanted to learn from another culture—one that was about the co-operation of the group rather than the achievements of the individual.

So, on October 4, 2011—exactly one year after ending my marriage—I set off for Tokyo. Unfortunately, this undertaking was a complete and immediate disaster. The job was not working at a single preschool as I had been led to believe. Instead, I was teaching in about twenty different locations all over Tokyo and Yokohama—an area with a population of about thirty-five million. I was expected to find each new location in a city I did not know, on a train system that is one of the most complicated in the world, with a map system that had no street names and was written in a language I did not speak. I was leaving my apartment two hours before work and was still unable to find the locations on time, and I was therefore shamed by my employers and colleagues for being a "lazy foreigner" who was always late.

The stress of this took a toll on my body. After a few weeks, I fell tremendously ill and almost died of pneumonia. I was hospitalized for a week, and upon leaving I was given a doctor's note ordering me to take two weeks of strict bedrest. I sent this note to my employer by registered mail because I was aware of their dislike of me. Yet when I returned to work on December 22, I was immediately fired by the woman who had hired me. Merry Christmas to me! On that day, I learned that doctor-ordered bedrest and being late due to struggling to find your workplace were both firing-worthy offences in Japan.

Upon hearing this news, my friends and family told me I should return to Canada. They had no concept of the hours of hell I had endured to get a foreign resident card, a Japanese bank account, and a Tokyo cell phone. I wasn't going to waste my suffering. I knew that Japan was where I was supposed to be, and that a miracle was on its way that would allow me to stay.

As it turned out, I was right. A few weeks later I was offered a job in the Shizuoka prefecture at the base of Mt. Fuji. This company and community were wonderfully good to me and became the foundation of my life in Japan. I was able to settle into a rural life among my students. Some were children, some were adults of all ages and vocations, many of who also became my personal friends. I was finally able to make my contributions to the world in a workplace where I was appreciated and esteemed. In my classes, I was able to have fascinating discussions with some of the greatest minds I had ever met and learn about one of the most incredible countries and cultures in the world.

Although this was a fascinating time of learning for me, it was also lonely and marked by personal tragedy. After spending my entire adult life married, I was adjusting to being alone and suffered greatly from the lack of companionship. Less than a year after arriving in Japan, I got skin cancer and had to have three surgeries that left my face temporarily disfigured. And then, shortly after my surgery, my brother died unexpectedly. Due to financial considerations and family tensions, I was unable to return to Canada and grieve his death with the people who loved him.

All of this was made more difficult by the fact that I had

very few people I could turn to for support. When you live alone in another country, especially one whose culture and language are so completely different from your own, the isolation can be overwhelming. In addition, I was enduring a campaign against me back in Canada. When a person finds the courage to unravel the puzzle of dysfunction within their lives and therefore stops playing their assigned role within their social group, it creates conflict that often results in them being rejected by the people they love. Most of my closest friends abandoned me, as did many of my family members; to them, I was the person in the wrong who was reaping the consequences of my selfish choices.

These experiences brought about a lot of deep sorrow, and I decided to feel every bit of it instead of numbing the pain through substances or escapism. I was fully and totally alive in that pain, and so I was able to experience some of the greatest beauty in my entire life. It kept me present and awakened to the exquisiteness that surrounded me—the fresh snow atop Mt. Fuji as I stepped outside in the mornings, the glory of flowers growing out of industrial ruins, the joy on a little child's face in response to a song played on my guitar. I believe that in the midst of our deepest losses, we can increase our awareness in order to see life's most miraculous wonders. And when we employ the determination and grit of resilience in times of great pain, we can begin to create a new reality of beauty and love for ourselves and for our loved ones.

During this time of sorrow, I discovered that there was only one person I could trust and rely on, and that person was me. I was the one who understood the reasons behind the decisions I had made. I was the one who understood my own brokenness and had compassion for my shortcomings. And I was the one who could decide that I was worthy of love, support, and comfort. In those moments, I decided that I was a beautiful person and a treasure to this world, and that I had my gifts of love and music to offer those whose path gave me an opportunity to do so.

This was a turning point for me. It no longer mattered how anybody else felt about me because I respected and admired myself. I had the fortitude it took to keep working, growing, and being of service in the midst of all of that pain and loss. I was stronger than any other person I knew, and I was proud of myself. I was making contributions to the lives of the people around me—to me, that is what mattered most.

It has been ten years since those darkest of days, and the life I have created for myself since is one of joy and service. I am back in Canada now and have a good relationship with my family members, who have also grown considerably since those difficult years. By taking myself out of the role I had played for so long, I gave them the opportunity to reassess themselves and their experiences within the dysfunctional system we had all endured. I now have wonderful, deep friendships that replaced the ones lost during that first year in Japan. I even have a handful of precious, gritty friends who refused to be turned against me. I have an amazing job in Tokyo at an international school whose owner and staff members have become some of my dearest friends, and I go to teach there whenever the opportunity arises—usually about three months per year.

I have written a lot of music since ending my marriage, and all that time spent alone helped me to grow considerably as a musician. It was never my dream to be a singer and songwriter; I only ever wanted to have a loving family life. Yet it is due to my failure to achieve my dream that my music has been created. I believe that we can turn tragedy into creative opportunity, and that is how I have sought to live my life—to always look for ways to create beauty amid whatever circumstances I find myself in. I am in the process of releasing my second album, and within it there is a song called "Love Found Me" that is a poetic autobiography about this journey. It has been a long and difficult road, but it feels as if everything I have surrendered has been returned to me with generosity and joy.

Most recently, I have fallen in love with a kind and supportive person who cares deeply for me. Finding love has been a long and arduous process—after the break-up of my marriage, I experienced several failed attempts at relationships that brought me some of the deepest heartbreak I have ever known. I would not wish the disappointments in love that I have endured upon my worst enemies. However, the pain from those moments became the inspiration for songs that I hope will bring the same comfort to others that they have brought to me.

I was only able to draw into my life the love and respect that I deserve once I found the deepest love and respect for myself in the midst of my greatest sorrows. By giving my losses the time and emotional attentiveness they required, I was able to pick up the pieces of myself and my circumstances and create what was possible. This isn't the life I had hoped or planned for, but it is one that has great beauty and contribution within it.

I could not be more proud of and grateful for the life of love I have created over these last ten years. I give thanks for every meaningful connection I have made, for every moment of joy or comfort I have participated in, and for all the learning and the growing I have done. I want this same strength and freedom for others, and I believe that comes from learning to love, respect, and admire ourselves even in the worst of circumstances. If, when tragedy strikes, we soberly bear our pain and carefully unravel the puzzle of why we are in those circumstances, our increased wisdom enables us to glean every single blessing offered by the sorrows of our lives. And most importantly, when we shamelessly persevere in our quest toward truth, love finds us.

Love Found Me
By Kristin Ormiston

Love found me, love found me underneath a thousand leaves,
love found me
Love found me, love has lifted us up into the trees
It's hard to believe but love found me

I took to the road to be alone,
I wandered the earth without any home
I wept an ocean and I loved a stone,
but love, love, love, found me

My friends turn to foes, when I stand my ground,
The shame bombs they launch, fall without any sound
I wept an ocean and I loved a stone,
but love, love, love, found me

About Kristin Ormiston

Arriving in the spring of 1969, Kristin Ormiston was an infant witness to several important historic events, including the first man on the moon and the Woodstock Music Festival. This would have a ripple effect that stretched out into the rest of her life. Kristin met Neil Armstrong at a leadership convention when she was nineteen years old, and her musical style has since been compared to Woodstock-era artists Joni Mitchell and Joan Baez.

Kristin's family has a history of mental illness, strong leadership, and a dash of obscure brilliance. This made growing up a complicated process. She has directed the energy resulting from these challenges into a quest for wisdom, and the reflections of her discoveries are shared through her songwriting.

Kristin has lived and performed all over the world, including seven years employed by Rosebud Theatre in Alberta and another seven at the Chemainus Theatre Festival in British Columbia. In 2011, she relocated to Tokyo where she eventually became the Artist in Residence at New World International School. She later returned to Canada, and in 2018 she began working and performing at Gather, a restaurant and live performance venue on Pender Island, BC, where she owns a hobby farm. Kristin's next album, *Love Found Me*, will be released in 2021.

Spotify: Kristin Ormiston
Apple Music: Kristin Ormiston
Facebook: facebook.com/Kristin-Ormiston-100341761537795

5

Manifesting Your Dreams

By Therese Lafleche

"A mind that is stretched by a new experience can never go back to its old dimensions."
Oliver Wendell Holmes

Manifesting Your Dreams

By Therese Lafleche

Mark Twain once wrote, "Travel is fatal to prejudice, bigotry, and narrow-mindedness, and many of our people need it sorely on these accounts. Broad, wholesome, charitable views of men and things cannot be acquired by vegetating in one little corner of the earth all one's lifetime." My personal experience has shown me just how true this statement is. When you continuously remove yourself from your comfort zone, you program yourself to accomplish anything and everything you set your mind to. This puts you in a space where your dreams can come true—often without you realizing it.

My obsession with travel began when I was six or seven years old and saw a globe for the very first time. I remember thinking to myself that the world is so small, and that life is so long. In that moment, I decided there was no way I would stay in my little corner of the world for my entire life. No matter how long it took, I was going to experience all the different cultures and learn from them. There was nothing that could stand in my way.

That day, a seed was planted that would grow into a life of travel and adventure—one filled with self-discovery, the man of my dreams, and a unique education for my children. For now, though, I was still just a child, and adulthood seemed so far away.

My desire to travel the world was completely unrealistic to my parents; they just considered it to be harmless daydreaming. I was often told "to get my head out of the clouds and my feet back on the ground" because I was setting myself up for disappointment. I never shared with them my thoughts about actually living in different parts of the world—I wanted one house on the ocean and another in the French countryside. In fact, I eventually stopped sharing all of my travel and adventure dreams with them, but I never stopped travelling the world in my mind. I remember spending countless nights laying in bed and imagining the Eiffel Tower, seeing the elegant ladies in their haute couture and drinking champagne in exquisite houses. I spent hours planning my beautiful home in the French countryside and thinking of the soirees I would host there.

As I grew up, my fantasies of France became a distant memory as I started to dream about going to Africa, Egypt, and other parts of Europe. I would travel through brochures and started my first bucket list.

Then, France came back into my life. During my first year of college, one professor taught us about the Chateau de Versailles in all its glory—this was where Louis XV reigned and had a love affair with Madame de Pampadour. In those times, kings married for political reasons and had mistresses for their personal pleasures. Louis XV had many, and Jeanne Antoinette Poisson hoped to become one of them. She attempted to catch his eye at various hunting events, and she succeeded. She was invited to a masked ball where the king publicly declared his affection for her and she then became his official mistress. Three months later, Louis purchased the title of "Marquise of Pompadour" so that she could be presented to the court. This was above and beyond the usual treatment of a mistress—an attestment to the love and respect he held for her. She later became known as prime minister due to her influence over politics and was a patron of the arts, among many other things. She was the only person whom Louis fully trusted and who could be counted on to tell him the truth. Their relationship was dear to him as she understood him like no other.

I remember getting goosebumps when we were shown an image of a room in his private apartment; there was something so special about the desk that stood within it. About a half hour into the lesson, we were told that this desk had a secret compartment where King Louis XV kept his love letters from Madame de Pompadour.

It's hard to explain, but that day something shifted in my way of thinking about love. The way he declared his feelings in front of so many people, the way she was treated like an equal, the closeness of their relationship... It was such a beautiful story.

After this lesson, I became somewhat obsessed with Versailles. I imagined myself walking the gardens and dancing in the Hall of Mirrors. Then, in 1996, I had my daughter Chelsea, and my thoughts of Versailles and France came to an end. I was now in the most incredible relationship I'd ever had in my life—I had always known I wanted children, but I had no idea of how overwhelming the love for one's child could be.

I now had my very own little princess to take care of, and as a single mother with no financial support, I was happy to keep my travels to far-away places within the pages of her books.

While we did not do any grand trips overseas, we did travel. We lived in Montreal for over a year, spent a few years in Mississauga and then Toronto, and then moved to Florida to warm up under the palm trees.

In January of 2007, one of my colleagues started telling me about his brother-in-law and what an incredible man he is. My coworkers had made several unsuccessful attempts at matchmaking before, so I can't say I was interested in the slightest. However, when I got to my office and turned on my computer, I found an email from this brother-in-law. Uwe introduced himself and told me a little about his life; he had a way of writing that made it feel like he was right there speaking with me. When I opened the attached picture, I found myself looking at a beautiful man with warm eyes wearing a sweater and sitting next to a fireplace. I don't know what it was exactly about the image, but something about it felt like home. I just knew somehow that my very own fairy tale was starting to take shape. There was only one problem: he was a German living in France, which is quite a long way from Florida.

Uwe and I spent the next few weeks writing back and forth several times a day. We spent our evenings together on Skype, and our connection grew with every conversation. There was something so natural about talking with him. I was being swept off my feet, and for the first time in my life I could imagine myself getting married—while I had always wanted children, the idea of marriage was not one that appealed to me until now.

After six weeks, I told him I wanted to go to France and meet him. I was a little nervous that we wouldn't click as well in person or there would be some sort of disappointment from one of us, but I told myself that I had nothing to lose. Worst-case scenario, I would have at least seen Paris.

As it turned out, I had nothing to worry about; everything about this trip was amazing. After Uwe picked me up from the airport, we drove along the Seine, had lunch at Fouquet's, and strolled down the Champs Elysées. We talked, laughed, and just soaked up the essence of each other all night and morning. After just being an image or voice for so long, it was like we were finally becoming real to each other.

The second day we had a picnic in the Jardins Tuileries outside the Louvre. Paris was everything I had imagined, and discovering it in this way, with this man, just made it so much more magical. Uwe was truly a prince and unlike anyone I had ever met. He opened doors and took my hand as I would get out of the car. He paid attention to every little detail and made sure that I felt like a princess. I felt like I was living a dream.

On the third morning, we drove to the Chateau de Versailles—the castle I had been so obsessed with was right there! I hadn't realised how close it was to Paris. I was about to spend the day visiting the gardens and Chateau I had been dreaming of since my first year of college with a man who had completely swept me off my feet. Could it get any better? YES! Without ever knowing that I had wanted to visit Versailles, Uwe chose this spot to propose to me.

We spent the rest of the afternoon exploring the castle and its grounds. At one point we were outside at the top of the stairs, looking down at the expansive gardens. Uwe was behind me with his arms wrapped around my waist, and in that instant I remembered how my idea of romance had shifted when I first learned of this incredible place—how wonderful it was to discover that love would find you regardless of situation or marital status. And now here I was in the very spot

I would fantasize about, caught up in an unlikely relationship: a Canadian living in Florida who had fallen in love with a German living in France.

After a magical week together, I went home to Chelsea. Uwe came and spent a few months with us, and then we flew back and forth for a while until, finally, Chelsea and I got everything in order and moved to France.

Soon after our move, another long-forgotten dream came true. Uwe and I bought our first home together: an eleventh-century watermill in the Loire Valley, just thirty minutes from Leonardo Da Vinci's last home, which was surrounded by vineyards and castles. One evening, we were having a dinner party and I ran out to the wine cellar. As I was walking back to the house, I realized it looked just like the home in the French countryside I used to dream about—the ivy covering the walls, all of the windows lit from within, laughter ringing out into the night. It was everything I had wanted and more, right down to the little waterfall that could be heard from the bedroom window. The feeling of gratitude that washed over me was so overwhelming; I felt like I could explode from happiness.

Uwe and I later created another fairy-tale moment here when we got married on the property. The red carpet was laid, an altar was built, and we were surrounded by our family and friends from around the world. Just five months after we said "I do," Chelsea's dream came true and she got the sibling she had been asking for since she was a child. We welcomed our son Jonathan into the world and became a complete family: mother, father, sister, and brother. Funny how this is something I had never envisioned for myself, yet as I sit here and write these words I have tears in my eyes from the joy it has brought me.

Not long after Jonathan was born, things began to change

in our family. Chelsea started an internship with a Michelin chef and moved out, and Uwe was spending quite a bit of time in Paris for work. Jonathan and I would go with him most of the time, but I knew this wasn't going to be possible once Jonathan started school. We still loved the property and house, but with nearly four acres of gardens it required a lot of time and work. I was also starting to get itchy feet and was ready for a new adventure. So, we packed up and moved to Germany. I was excited to get to know a new culture and thought it would be great to be close to Uwe's family.

After this move, I realised just how important travel had always been to me; there is something within me that seems to require it. The thought of being in just one place for the rest of my life actually gives me a sensation similar to claustrophobia. It's like I can feel the oxygen being sucked out of the room, and I get a mild feeling of panic.

Once we were in Germany, I started teaching English to business executives and owners. It was the perfect opportunity to get to know the different traditions of this county, but it was far from being my dream job. Then I decided to bring a few students on an English language retreat where I could immerse them in the language and give them a holiday at the same time. Not only did this give me the opportunity to travel, but the students also learned more in one week than they normally did after months of lessons. This was the birth of my language retreats and business. As exciting as it was, I felt a little like an imposter in the world of languages and knew that there had to be a way to make a living out of my passion.

This is when I first came across that quote by Mark Twain, and it made me realize that what I really wanted, what would truly make me feel fulfilled, was to find a way to bring cultures together.

We were in Germany during the big refugee crisis in 2015, and seeing such deep-seated religious beliefs come together and find a way to co-exist was a truly priceless education for both Jonathan and me. We saw how easy it is to become prejudiced against a certain group and how quickly that prejudice dissipates as soon as you gain an understanding of where the other person comes from, why they do things the way they do, and what they believe. We are all fundamentally the same; skin colour, language, religious beliefs, and traditions are simply the spices in life.

The things I have learned about myself, finding my husband and creating my family, teaching my children about different cultures and religions—none of this would have happened if I had never travelled. My children have knowledge and opinions that they have made themselves through their lived experiences rather than just through pictures in a book and the perspectives of whichever author they may be reading in school.

Now here we are at the end of 2020 and, regardless of where you live in the world, I think we can all agree this has been a year like no other. It has been a year of social distancing and learning how to do things differently. A year without much travel, and for some, without work. A year of not being able to spend time with family or go to mass. While this has been frustrating, we all have the choice of seeing the glass as being half full or half empty. We can see this as a year of obstacles or a year of opportunities.

I have decided to be grateful and look at the accomplishments I have made during this extremely strange time. My family and I managed to move from Germany back to France and discovered an area that we previously had no interest in and yet turned out to have everything we were looking for. We bought a house here just a few minutes' walk from the ocean. I shifted my business and am now helping people discover France from their home, and as a result I made some new friends and was invited to participate in this book.

As I sat in my garden one day and thought about all of these blessings, I started feeling much better about the year. And in that moment, much like the moment at the watermill, I realised where I was sitting. You see, my backyard is surrounded by a tall, ancient stone wall. At the top of the garden are a couple menhirs, and I was currently sitting on a dolmen. These stones are found in various parts of Asia, Africa, and western Europe, but the largest and oldest formations are right here in Brittany, France. Some date back to two thousand years before the pyramids were built.

I had an immediate flashback to college, when I was fascinated by the Egyptians and their history—the pyramids, the mystery surrounding the burial chambers, and the energy attached to the stones. I really wanted to experience this for myself. It wasn't just a thought or a fleeting wish; it was something physical, almost spiritual. I would actually see myself standing at the foot of a pyramid and looking up at this monolithic structure. I could feel the coolness of the stone and the awe of being in the presence of something so mystical.

Without knowing it, I had once again made my dream come true despite having forgotten about it for decades. I may not have visited the pyramids and felt the energy attached to those stones, at least not yet, but instead I found myself giving gratitude for my life while sitting on my very own dolmen—a stone far older and perhaps even more mystical. I get shivers as I think about it, and my face turns into a large grin.

Someone once told me how impressive it was that I had made my dreams come true, and my response was quite ridiculous: "But I didn't. They just sort of happened. I didn't have a plan, no checklist, I didn't even have a vision board in place." As soon as I said this, I realised that even though acheiving these dreams wasn't planned, I had the most important ingredients: a strong desire to experience them and no considerations that they couldn't or wouldn't happen. Then I just let go, and the universe took care of the rest.

My dreams have come true for me so many times, and I know yours have for you as well—we just don't always realise it. We usually have our vision so fixated on the future that we don't realise the magic we have created in the present. So take this opportunity to think of your own dream. Close your eyes and really project yourself into it. See it, smell it, and most of all, believe it and get excited about it. Then, let it go. Keep yourself open to opportunities and experiences and let the universe do the rest.

We are capable of so much more than we give ourselves credit for. And when we put our overthinking aside, when we take our focus off of the future and learn to enjoy the present, we create magic and make our dreams come true.

About Therese Lafleche

Therese Lafleche has been travelling and moving to new countries since the age of seventeen. She has done so as a young woman, as a single mother, and now with her husband and son. She believes that travel is the best education one can get and is the perfect way to relax, discover yourself, and grow as a person.

As the founder of Passport Lifestyles, she has a vision of bringing cultures together through language and travel. She has been offering language and cultural retreats since 2017 and is now inviting you to get the full experience of France from the comfort of your own home. Within her membership group, you will get to know the history and culture of France; discover hidden gems, hot spots, fashion, and travel tips; and receive insider tours and special offers from French artists and merchants. You will also have access to live cooking classes with a chef in Paris as well as language lessons. Once you know which areas intrigue you the most, she can customize a retreat for you or you can join one of the planned retreats.

www.passportlifestyles.fr
Email: therese@passportlifestyles.fr

6

Like Mother, Like Daughter

By Angel Baney

"A daughter will follow in her mom's footsteps so make sure to set a good example."
Elizabeth George

Like Mother, Like Daughter

By Angel Baney

Throughout my life, there have been many obstacles and challenges that impacted my self-esteem and self-worth. However, I had done a lot of work on myself in preparation for the birth of my daughter, Gianna, and I thought I had left it all behind. It wasn't until earlier this year that I realized I wasn't completely healed. Like an onion, I had layers that needed to be peeled back to reveal the scars that were embedded deep in my tissue.

This realization began in March of 2020, when all the schools shut down due to the pandemic. Gianna's class switched to remote learning within a week, and I believed she would have no problem adjusting to this. She knew how to work the computer, and as an only child I thought she would definitely want to see her classmates. I set our living room up just like her classroom, and I provided books and folders to keep her assignments organized. I thought she was ready to go. I was wrong.

Remote learning quickly became a nightmare. Gianna refused to listen to her teachers and would even refuse to turn her camera on so that she could perform gymnastics instead of paying attention. I became incredibly frustrated. Instead of trying to discuss it with her, I would start to scream at her, asking why she was doing this to me. The screaming often turned into fighting and slamming doors, and both of us would end up crying.

At this same time, my over twenty-year career as a bodyworker and movement specialist came to an end after the pandemic forced my business to close. It was a difficult decision, but it did have a positive effect in that it allowed me to focus on a new career path I had been exploring. Prior to the shutdown, I had enrolled in several classes on communication and personality science as I wanted to become a relationship coach. My internal goal was to help moms give their daughters a voice by teaching them communication skills that would help them to speak out against bullying and abuse without shame or guilt.

The classes started in March, and within a few weeks they provided me with the holy grail that would change my relationship with my daughter. I learned that her dominant personality was the opposite of mine, and that this was the source of our conflict. I want love and peace but also structure and a system for her to get things done; she wants freedom and flexibility, not structure. I had to step into her shoes and find ways to make her realize she had a lot of opportunities for fun once her work was completed. In turn, I had to be willing to step out of my structure and be more flexible.

As I examined our interactions, I was brought back to my childhood. I remembered that when I was her age, fighting and screaming were a regular occurrence within my family home. I was falling into the pattern of what I had experienced growing up, and I knew that I could not let this situation continue—not only for my own benefit, but also for my seven-year-old as well. There had to be a better way. To find the answer, I needed to take a closer look at my past.

I want to begin by saying that I do not see myself as a victim of my childhood, and I do not blame my parents for anything that happened. They were very loving and encouraged us to do everything we wanted to. However, they also grew up in environments that taught them certain ways they should behave as parents, and not all of those ways were positive.

My parents fought many times throughout my childhood, mostly over money. My mother expressed to us many times that we never had enough, an opinion that was driven by the fact that the people in the next neighbourhood over were much richer than us. They had bigger houses and nicer cars. They went out to nicer restaurants and dressed much better. My mom felt pressured to keep up, so she would take us shopping and buy the best clothes and shoes for us to wear, spending money we didn't have. When the credit card bill came in, the fighting would ensue. My father was more passive aggressive, so he would eventually switch to ignoring Mom, which then made her scream louder to get his attention. The fighting grew even louder as I grew older, with crying and slamming doors becoming a regular pattern. And through this experience, the impression that we never had enough became stuck in my tissue—a false realty that I would bring into my adult years.

By the time I was in seventh grade, the level of communication in our house dropped to the point that it was nonexistent. My mom had been a stay-at-home mom up until this point; now that my siblings and I were old enough to take care of ourselves, she got a job as an accountant in a law firm to bring in some extra income. She was always busy cleaning, cooking, or working, and when we did spend time together it was often outside with friends. We did not speak a lot at the dinner table, and the conversations we did have were short as we were all so busy with our own activities. Our communication further reduced when I began coming home so late from swim practice that I missed having dinner with the family. I would get home, eat by myself, and just go to bed. As a result, I became very independent from my family. I turned to my friends for advice, and I stopped asking my parents for things I needed because I felt they were both too busy.

In my sophomore year, I ended up in a lot of the same classes my older sister had taken. Her IQ was much higher than mine, yet I was expected to be just as good at everything. The teachers constantly compared me to her. Why wasn't I as smart as she was? Why didn't I write as well as she did? Even my friends compared the two of us. I heard over and over again how amazing she was, and I thought that meant I was not. My self-esteem hit an all-time low. I decided to quit all sports because I wasn't going to get a scholarship or make a career out of them. I then got a job so that I didn't have to ask my parents for money, especially as a recent investment had left them financially devastated, and my work became an excuse for not doing well in school.

That year I also met Joe, who was two years older than me, and we dated up until my senior year. He was loyal and loving but didn't talk much—I realize now that I was attracted to him because he was similar to my dad. He didn't compliment me, so when he invited me to his prom I decided I had to improve my appearance. I had gained quite a bit of weight since I quit swimming, so I started using a dietary supplement to speed things up. It soon became a bad habit, making me lose all the weight I wanted to and then some, but I kept taking it until my senior year of high school for fear of gaining back what I had lost.

At the end of my senior year, I was accepted to a college in a completely different state than the one my sister was attending. I thought this meant my life would improve because I wouldn't be compared to her anymore, and at first it was great. However, I was taking difficult classes because I wanted to be a marine biologist, and I was working two jobs to pay my loans which made it hard to study. As a result, my grades were good but not excellent. In my second year, the classes became even more challenging. I had an organic chemistry class that I loved, but after studying so hard for the test, I received a D+. I began to think I was a failure, that I was stupid, and that I shouldn't have gone to college.

Then second semester tuition came due, and after paying it I didn't have enough in my account to cover another semester. I decided to take on another job, but trying to keep up with classes while working three jobs turned out to be unsustainable. So, I dropped out. I was too ashamed to admit to my parents that I was working three jobs to make ends meet, so instead I lied and said I had quit because I wanted to move to Boston. I had started seeing someone who lived there and, since it's close to the ocean, I claimed it would be easier for me to pursue my dream of being a marine biologist in this city. At least, that's what I told them.

I didn't return to school after getting settled in Boston, and this was a huge disappointment to my parents. Every time I called them, the first thing they would say to me was how I should go back to college. But the more they said this, the more determined I became to prove I could be successful without a degree. The first job I found was at an upscale Italian family restaurant, and I worked many hours and learned quickly on the job so I could make more money. Within months, I had moved up into a management position and was taking home a great paycheck.

Unfortunately, things were not going as well within my relationship. My boyfriend was attending classes to become a paramedic and spent his nights riding in an ambulance, so we didn't see each other much. One day, I was cleaning out his bag to do his laundry and found love notes to his old girlfriend. I was devastated. He told me nothing had happened—that she was moving away, and since they had been together a long time he needed to say goodbye. I forgave him and we stayed together, but the trust was broken.

Two years later, Kenny—a chef I had met at work— approached me with an opportunity. He wanted to start a catering and deli business and thought I would be an ideal partner. I said yes, and soon I was working day and night to make our business successful. And once again, my relationship took a downturn. My boyfriend cheated for the second time a year later, and this time I didn't forgive. We only had a month left on our lease, and as the person making all the money and paying all the bills, I told him to go back home and live with his mother. Then I explained everything that was going on to my business partner and his girlfriend, and they invited me to stay with them until I found another place. I didn't realize that I was putting myself in a very awkward situation until it was too late.

Kenny and I didn't pay ourselves much out of our business, which meant there was no way I could save enough to move out. After several months, Kenny's girlfriend decided she couldn't stay if he wouldn't kick me out; when he refused to do so, she left. I had no intention of getting involved with him, but he was incredibly charming, and I soon found myself falling for him. He told me he loved me and wanted to start a family with me, and I believed him. I had no idea what was to come.

One night, Kenny drank too much and started to blame me for the hard times we were encountering. He grabbed me by the wrist and bent my fingers back; the pain was awful, and I knew at least one if not all were broken. I waited for him to pass out, then grabbed what little I owned and drove eight hours to Pittsburgh. I didn't tell my parents what happened, only that we had fought and that I was reconsidering coming home. Kenny called day and night begging me to come back, claiming he didn't mean to hurt me and that he didn't remember what he'd done. After three days, I agreed to return and drove back to Boston. This was in part because I was taught to be loyal, and because we had a business that I needed to get back to. But in truth, I also couldn't stand being at home. My parents kept telling me that I was better off in Pittsburgh, that I could live with them and go back to school. My mom also continually insisted that I would be nothing without an education. That was the final straw; I decided I had to go back and prove them wrong.

The next five years were filled with emotional, sexual, and physical abuse. I was cut off from our finances, I didn't own a car, I didn't have friends, and I didn't speak with my family as often. My whole life revolved around work and home, which meant Kenny and I were with one another 24/7. The emotional abuse left scars deep within my tissue and made me believe I couldn't do anything. That I was worthless. That I had to stay loyal, even in an abusive situation.

In 1997, Kenny and I lost everything due to his episodes of drinking and disappearing for days. We had to move back to Pittsburgh because it was the only place we could start over; my parents were willing to take us in until we got jobs and found our own place. I began working at a car dealership while Kenny found a job as a chef. Now that weren't working together, his anger heightened because he could no longer control me. Soon the physical abuse became so bad that I knew he would eventually kill me if I stayed with him—he had already attempted to several times.

At this point, I had a good support system in place. I now had friends I had met through work, and I was able to confide in them about the abuse. I was promoted at the dealership and was making the most money I had ever earned, and I had opened a secret account where I tucked money away. Also, my relationship with my parents had changed—I didn't tell them everything that was going on, but they saw how successful I was at work and celebrated my achievements. They realized I had been through tough times, and that I had endured. I no longer felt ashamed and worthless in their eyes. Finally, I was given the permission I felt I needed from my parents: they told me I didn't have to be loyal to Kenny, and I didn't have to stay with him. With that, I stopped being a victim and left.

Since that day, my life has improved dramatically. In 1999, after Kenny went back to Boston, I had enough money saved to find a career that resonated with me. I wanted to do something that had meaning, and I felt a desire to help people. So, I went back to school to become a bodyworker and movement specialist. I worked as a waitress throughout the nine-month program so I could pay for school and save money, and I paid off all my debt within a year of graduating.

I then met and married Tom, my present husband, who is

a wonderful man. We wanted to start a family, so I did a lot of work on myself to prepare for motherhood—I knew that we were going to have to see fertility specialists due to the damage Kenny had done to my pelvic area. And after ten years and four fertility clinics, we had our daughter on December 21, 2012. The day she was born was the most amazing day of my life.

During my fertility journey, I saw a doctor who specialized in a type of energy work called cellular healing as well as acupuncture and natural medicine. She helped me believe that I was good enough to conceive and that I deserved to be a mom, allowing me to rid myself of the rhetoric of not being good enough that Kenny had buried deep within my tissues. I began to mediate and use affirmations to let my mind and heart connect to my womb. I also exercised several times a week and improved my nutrition, all in preparation for our baby.

The work that I did before Gianna arrived helped me deal with the years of abuse I had endured and the self-esteem issues created by my childhood experiences. However, it wasn't until I began working towards becoming a relationship coach that I recognized I was "becoming my mother" by mimicking her habits, and that I still had unresolved issues around my upbringing. I realized that I cannot repeat the patterns I observed in my own childhood—the negativity, the disappointed body language, the yelling, the lack of communication. I needed to make a change.

Learning, speaking, and living the B.A.N.K.™ methodology—a personality coding system designed to help you communicate with and understand the people around you—improved my relationship with my daughter dramatically. I have learned the words that trigger her to get things done and the words that create a negative response. There are still the beginnings of meltdowns, but I am now able to stop them before they become out of control.

I believe that we must break the patterns of our mother's parenting—but in order to do this, we first must be willing to recognize it. We must bring our unconscious trauma to our conscious mind so that we can deal with it and move past it. And once we do this, we can begin teaching our daughters a new way of being. We can take the time to understand them by stepping into their shoes and looking at the world through their eyes. We can learn to communicate with our daughters, something we should do by the time they turn six—research has shown girls lose their self-confidence and their voice by the time they are eight. And we can empower them to use their voice and to stand up against bullying and abuse. By doing this, we create a whole new pattern, a new cycle, that will ripple through generations of women to come.

About Angel Baney

For over twenty years, Angel Baney held a career as a bodyworker and movement specialist. In that time, she opened up several spas and served as a teaching assistant for one of the top massage therapist leaders in the world. She also treated rescue workers in Pennsylvania and New York while they were searching for survivors of the 9/11 tragedy, and the massage chair she used is now part of history at the Smithsonian Institute in Washington, DC.

In March 2020, Angel pivoted her career after the world shut down due to the pandemic. She is now a certified B.A.N.K.™ IOS Coach and is licensed to teach B.A.N.K.™ relationships and fundamentals. Her passion is to help mothers communicate with their preteen daughters so they can build strong bonds. Angel also serves on her daughter's school board and chairs the parent-teacher committee. She is passionate about helping her community and both fundraises for and donates to several charities.

Angel currently lives in Pittsburgh, Pennsylvania with her husband Tom. She has one daughter and three cats. Most of her immediate family lives in Pittsburgh, and they enjoy spending time getting together.

www.hearmyvoicenow.com

7

Happily Ever After—Interrupted

By Sarah Voth

"Happiness is not something ready made. It comes from your own actions."
Dalai Lama

Happily Ever After—Interrupted

By Sarah Voth

A few years ago, I came across an inspiring poem by Veronica A. Shoffstall called "After a While." The following verse struck me and burrowed its way into my psyche: "After a while you learn that even sunshine burns if you get too much. So you plant your own garden and decorate your own soul, instead of waiting for someone to bring you flowers." The poem describes how there are no promises in life, but you can learn and grow from every goodbye. It is a poem that speaks almost directly to my own personal experience and to the lessons I learned along the way.

I was fifteen when I met and began seeing my very first boyfriend. His family was very strong in their Christian faith, and I slowly came on board. Together, we formed a faith-based relationship. When we were both twenty-three, we married and began our happily ever after—or so I thought. I was very naïve and believed without a doubt that no matter what the future had in store, I would spend my life with this man. That was my first misconception and my first lesson: there is no guarantee of a "happily ever after."

Because we married so young, we continued to mature together; sadly, we were not heading in the same direction. For the first while, though, things were good. We were fortunate to have two amazing children, and we were plugging along among the chaos of a household with two working parents. But as the years passed, life became more challenging and the differences in our parenting and lifestyle choices began to show. I've always had this overbearing sense of duty, so when things need to be done, I do them. Kids' soccer teams needed coaching? I did it. Car pools needed to be organized and run? I did it. School volleyball team needed someone to facilitate, as did the track and field program? I did it, all while working full time. The more I did, the less time there was for our relationship, and it soon became clear that my husband and I were growing apart. However, as a Christian I believed that this was my calling and that I would be given the strength to make it through these tough times. So, I pushed on, determined to keep my "happily ever after."

Then, after seventeen years of marriage, my husband admitted to me that he had been unfaithful. I was completely blindsided. This doesn't happen in a Christian marriage, and it certainly doesn't happen to me! My husband loved me and had promised to do so forever. He had repeatedly said that he could never live without me, that he was nothing without me and the kids. These words were embedded in my mind and had kept me moving forward despite our differences. I never once doubted his faithfulness; I would have sworn to anyone that he would never cheat on me. Apparently, I was wrong.

Prior to his confession, he had been stricken with some serious panic attacks and was struggling to carry on with his daily activities—little did I know that this was a physiological reaction to what he had done. Even after hearing the truth, I continued to be the caregiver as he fell apart, becoming visibly broken and ashamed. I had to watch out for him and take care of the children without letting them know even a hint of what was going on.

When I met with my pastor shortly after the reveal, he asked me what I wanted to do. Despite what had happened, there was no question in my mind that I was going to stay. I felt it was my duty to hang on and fix this. This was my marriage, my life, and our kids needed a family. This would not break us. My husband and I went to counselling and talked through why the affair happened, how we could rebuild our relationship, and how we could re-establish trust and be aware of each other's needs. We even participated in a couple's weekend that was specifically designed for Christian marriages and tried to "unpeel the layers of the onion," as they called it. We were able to temporarily bandage the wound over time, but things never felt the same. As the saying goes, once trust is broken—especially the blind, naïve trust I'd had in this man and in our future—it is very difficult to get it back.

The fact that affection and intimacy were what he needed most in a relationship made our path to healing extremely challenging. These were out of the question for me for quite some time as all I could think about was what he had done with someone else. I tried to change how I felt, tried to forgive him, but it was so hard. My belief in him had been shattered; I had lost my respect for him as a husband. We grew further and further apart, especially as he withdrew into late nights out with friends and a couple of other "close female relationships" that didn't help the situation. We were broken, and as much as I was willing to hang on, he was not.

He had been seeing a counsellor on his own throughout this time and eventually asked me to come with him to an appointment. I thought this was where we would start working on rebuilding our relationship—nope, wrong again. During the session, the counsellor turned to him and asked, "Do you still love Sarah?" My husband stared at me and shrugged his shoulders, saying, "I don't know anymore." Excuse me? Once again, I was utterly shocked. This was not part of the "happily ever after" program either. Love was forever; *he* was the one who said so!

I sat in silence on that couch for a good ten minutes, just trying to breathe. This couldn't be happening. This was NOT happening. This man had sworn to love me forever. He'd said he'd never leave me. He'd said he couldn't live without me. He'd promised me we would never be a part of those divorce statistics. This was my life's plan, and there wasn't any other path to follow.

I don't remember the drive home that night or much about the days that followed.

The plan was for him to move out on his own, so we needed to tell the kids he was leaving. I insisted that he would have to be the one to explain the situation to them as this was his choice. But when we sat on the couch with our eight-year-old and twelve-year-old, he just began sobbing. The kids were confused and asked why Daddy was crying, so once again I pulled up my big girl pants and told them myself—not everything, just that things weren't going well and Daddy wasn't happy. That he needed some time away.

We quickly put the house up for sale and he moved into a one-bedroom apartment. Once the house sold, the kids and I went to stay with my sister until we could find a place of our own. I will be completely honest here: those first months were a disaster. I could go into great detail about my completely devastated and shattered life, about the wrongs committed against me and my children, but that would not be helpful. I will also say that I am not proud of how I handled the situation; I definitely did not take the high road. The advice around separation and divorce is that you should keep everything from the children and maintain an amicable relationship with the other parent. The emphasis is put on co-parenting in a positive way so that your kids feel loved, safe, and still part of a family. I totally agree with this concept, but I failed miserably at implementing it. I was so hurt and broken that I could barely speak to my soon-to-be ex, let alone look at his new partner. He wanted everything to be so smooth and comfortable between us all, but I struggled to maintain my composure every time I had to speak with him or see him around the neighbourhood living his new "best life." I wish I could have done better, but sometimes I just couldn't see through the pain. I forgive myself now, knowing that I did what I was capable of at the time.

I would never have made it through the devastation of this separation without the love and support of my family and so many amazing friends. I don't know how many times my sister had to drive over and pull me out of the bedroom closet or listen to me wailing on the phone because I had just seen him with "her" at our son's soccer game. My parents would have us come over on weekends and would treat the kids to special outings so that they could have fun while I had some time to grieve. Friends came to sit with me and told me that I would make it through this and be stronger for it. My girlfriend said something that, although harsh, made a lot of sense to me: "You can't go around the pain, you just have to go through it."

She was so right; there was no way around this, and it was going to hurt. Fortunately, I did not have to go through it alone.

This overabundance of care, love, and support brings me to my second lesson: you need a life outside your marriage and your duties as a mom. I had become so involved in my kids' lives and in being a wife that I hadn't allowed enough time for myself. I hadn't carved out any time to enjoy the relationships I had built with my friends and other important family members. I had let myself be overcome by "family duty" and had denied myself the opportunity to be my own person. Thank goodness my family and friends were still there for me when my world fell apart. I honestly would not have made it through this horrible time without them.

I have come to understand that your life cannot be defined by your significant other and your kids. You need to know that you are still loved, valued, and appreciated by the people who are important to you. Those relationships are every bit as crucial as your connection with your immediate family, and they must be nurtured.

About a year after my husband left, a friend forced me to join an online dating site, and I began my journey into the world of dating. That same friend actually sat in her car in the restaurant parking lot while I, at forty-two years old, went on my first date—ever. How scary is that! I was a nervous wreck, but I was surprised and flattered to hear the man say from across the table, "You are very beautiful." That right there was enough for me to consent to another date. I hadn't been complimented like that in such a long time, and it really impacted me. When someone chooses to leave you, your self-esteem goes into the toilet. You can't help but see all your faults on a daily basis and wonder how you could ever be appreciated by someone again. Hearing someone call me beautiful started to heal that wound, although I still had a long path to recovery ahead of me.

I got involved in a few other relationships after that one and was lured into each one by the overflow of compliments I received. It was amazing how someone's praise, affection, and flattery could have such an effect on me. If they doled it out, I took it. I just wanted someone to make me feel valued again. To feel wanted. To feel special. My desperation to find some self-worth resulted in a number of toads joining the list of suitors, and I do have some regrets about reacting so willingly to their offers of affection. I finally hit my turning point when I got involved with a guy who was seven inches shorter than me and ended up dumping me because I made him feel emasculated! I mean really, how low had I sunk?

You can probably guess that I took a long break from dating after this. I wanted to focus on myself, my work, my kids, and my family and friends. That's all I needed. I became the third wheel on many occasions as well as the "single girl" at parties, but I was okay with that. I learned that I didn't need to be attached to anyone to meet new people, have fun, or be adventurous. I got brave and began to embrace my independence. I still hoped to find love one day, but I was beginning to see that I needed to be okay on my own before I could be okay with somebody else—a dear friend had told me this a long time ago, but I didn't quite understand it until now.

This was my third lesson: I had to be the one who placed value on myself. I realized that I had been so drawn in by the compliments and words of praise coming from other men because I had been relying on them for my self-worth. Unless someone else said I was amazing, I just wasn't. Now I know that it is up to me, and ONLY me, to find my happiness and feel good about myself. I had to love me first before anyone else could; giving this power to someone else is a failure in the making.

As I learned to find my own self-worth, I asked myself, what can I do to make myself happy? What can I do to feel good about myself? Notice I am saying "what can *I* do" and not "what can *someone else* do." I started listing the things I loved doing—reading, art, exercising, hiking, dinner with the girls—and began putting those things into my schedule. I joined a gym and fell in love with a community of people who valued both mental and physical health above all else. It was hard in the beginning as my self-esteem was still fragile, but I persevered and am now feeling much healthier and stronger. I also explored interests such as crafting and painting and took courses in both. And as my world began to open up, I started to feel good about myself and what I was doing for ME.

After a while, I decided I was ready to try meeting someone again. This time, though, I knew I had to go into it with a very different attitude. I didn't *need* anyone; I just wanted to meet new people and enjoy the experience. I went online again—at my age, there are no single men just hanging about—and ended up connecting with a man who was very kind and genuine and didn't instantly shower me with compliments. We laughed and had fun together, but we did not move immediately into an exclusive, see-you-everyday type of relationship. Instead, this happened slowly over time and through a variety of activities and outings. I remember telling myself not to be looking for this person to be "the one"—that I was enjoying myself, but I was still happy on my own.

As it turns out, he *was* "the one," and we have now been together for over five years. We share the same beliefs and goals in life, and he possesses my two most favourite qualities:

kindness and a sense of humour. We love being together but value spending time with family and friends. We love travelling and have done some pretty adventurous things I never saw myself doing, including climbing a waterfall in Jamaica, swimming with stingrays in the Cayman Islands, and ziplining in Whistler. For a girl who's afraid of heights and slimy things with tails, this is pretty amazing! I appreciate how he shows his love for me through what he does, not what he says. He loves my kids, my family, and my crazy dog. He's taken it all on, and trust me, that's no easy feat! He cooks, he cleans, and he handles my anxiety and, let's just say it, my drama. There have been some difficult times, but we have supported each other through them all and have worked through the occasional road bump. Most importantly, we both have our own lives outside of our relationship.

I sometimes have to look back and remind myself of the lessons I've learned, but I think I'm still doing a pretty good job of staying in charge of my own happiness and knowing I will be okay, even if I have to be on my own. It's not always easy, and there are times when I slip into the routine of focusing only on my job, my kids, and any other duties I feel called to. That being said, I can now recognize when this is happening and make a conscious effort to do something for myself—something that brings me joy.

So, am I now the perfect woman with the perfect life? Far from it! However, I am stronger, wiser, and much more independent. I understand that life is full of lessons if you choose to look for them and learn from them. I have let go of my vision of a "happily ever after" and instead am focused on enjoying the "now" and ensuring that I have a life of my own to turn to no matter what. I have learned how important my friends and family are to me and that making time for them is a gift I give myself. I know that I am worthy of self-love and self-care, and that nobody can provide that for me but me.

Putting the key to my happiness in someone else's pocket will only lead to disappointment. As the poem says, I get to "plant my own garden and decorate my own soul"—no more waiting for someone else to do it.

About Sarah Voth

Sarah graduated from the University of British Columbia with a Bachelor of Arts and a Bachelor of Education. She has been teaching in the French immersion program for the last twenty-eight years and is passionate about her craft and the students she works with.

Sarah has experienced the pain and growth that comes from divorce and writes about her personal journey in this book. She wants to share her story in hopes that it might support others on this difficult road. She also wants to impart some of the valuable lessons she learned along the way—lessons that might help those currently in relationships.

8

Turning Poison into Medicine

By Heather Ann McBride

"A great human revolution in just a single individual will help achieve a change in the destiny of a nation and, further, can even enable a change in the destiny of all humankind."
Daisaku Ikeda

Turning Poison into Medicine

By Heather Ann McBride

In 2011, I was asleep in the back of a souped-up Subaru STI with a young coworker at the wheel and his girlfriend in the front passenger seat. The three of us had just enjoyed a day of snowboarding on the Willamette Pass, deep in the Cascade Mountains of Oregon. Well, Brandon and Stephanie snowboarded. I rolled around in the snow trying to flip over every time I fell, which was about every two minutes.

While we drove home on the mountain highway, the wind blew wildly through the trees. I laid my head back, drifting in and out of consciousness, watching the branches sway in the crazy wind. Then I heard Brandon say, "Look at that!" The tension in his voice shook me awake.

About two hundred yards ahead, a large old growth tree slowly toppled across the highway as a car drove under its falling trunk, narrowly avoiding being crushed. The behemoth slammed down on the black surface and split in half. Our car skidded to a stop and jolted in reverse. Thank goodness for the quick reactions of a young person and the extremely responsive brake system installed in the car just the day before.

Unbeknownst to us, another tree was suffering the same fate. I looked out the left window and saw the massive trunk, wider than our car, falling toward us. Right as it hit the roof, Brandon managed to pull forward just enough to prevent all three of us from being crushed. Instead, the tree smashed the entire back end of the car, landing right behind where I was sitting.

I will never forget my own screams as I witnessed even more trees falling around us, but those visions were actually trauma-induced illusions. My panicked state was broken when Brandon calmly turned around and asked, "Why are you screaming? It's over." I stopped the hysterics, but I was skeptical that we were truly safe. It was still windy, and those wonder-of-the-world trees I had been enjoying a few moments ago now looked like hideous monsters ready to smash me like a pancake.

To this day, ten years later, I won't drive through the forests of Oregon when there is a forecasted storm. And although I still love trees, I have gained a healthy respect for their tremendous destructive talents and will forever be scanning for potential attackers while in their presence. I can still see that large trunk falling toward us in my mind's eye as if it just happened yesterday.

After the accident, the three of us crawled over the first felled tree in the rain and took refuge in an eighteen-wheeler stuck on the other side. In a matter of moments, a large truck equipped with the biggest chainsaw I have ever seen cut right through the tree that landed on our car, effortlessly pushing both halves to the side of the road. I watched as the worker jumped out of his truck to inspect the road, then froze in his tracks when he noticed the destroyed vehicle. As he slowly crept towards the wreckage, I knew what he was thinking: "There are dead people in that car." Never have I understood the phrase "my life flashed in front of my eyes" until that moment.

My life changed that day. Before the accident, my reaction to "bad things" happening was an accumulation of reasons to be afraid and claim any phobia as my own. Anyone who knew me would have thought this event would become another fear added to my list. "Trees are my enemy. Check."

That day was different. That day, I felt freed from fear. I felt invincible, like I could do anything my heart desired! If I could survive a tree that most certainly saw a bullseye on my head, along with everything else that had already happened in my life (which is a whole story in itself), then maybe I really did have guardian angels—or *Shoten Zenjin*, as we call them in Nichiren Buddhism. We also believe that we can change any poison into medicine and that every obstacle is an opportunity for victory in our lives. To show *actual proof* in my faith, I went back to the mountain pass two weeks later and skied down a mountain for the first time ever. It was so empowering. For several months I went about doing whatever I wanted and didn't have a care in the world. I held difficult conversations I used to avoid. I took a week-long road trip through the Southwest desert and Death Valley, a vast expanse of heat I would never have visited before. I didn't even hold onto my arm rest when someone else was driving over the speed limit.

But then my fears started creeping back into my neurological net, and I asked myself, "Why am I so afraid again?" This time, however, the fear felt different. It was as if

I was standing outside of my body observing this frightened entity, unable to recognize who she was anymore.

> *"I'm scared of swimming in the sea*
> *Dark shapes moving under me"*
> **Peter Gabriel**

About the same time my old friend fear came knocking on my door again, my uncle Bruce Ricker died rather suddenly. He had been a filmmaker, director, and producer of jazz films who had collaborated with Clint Eastwood on *Johnny Mercer: The Dream's On Me* and many other documentaries. When a film festival in California wanted to honour my uncle's life, I was asked to create a ten-minute memorial video that would be shown prior to an awards ceremony. Even though I didn't know how to edit footage, I accepted the task because there was no one else to do it. I asked my friend Arden, an editor by trade, to help me get it done. It turned out to be a great little introduction to the essence of Bruce's work. And in the process, I caught the film bug!

A few months later, my aunt Kate gave me Bruce's camera equipment and tripod as she knew I was an aspiring writer who dabbled in screenwriting. I was honoured to be given Bruce's equipment, even though it felt a little daunting. How could I carry on his work? I only had an elementary understanding of how to cobble footage together and had written a screenplay that was dead in the water. I didn't know jack about filmmaking!

Then I watched the documentary *I Am* by Tom Shadyack, and it gave me a crazy idea. Tom is a film director well known for his comedy film work with Jim Carrey in movies such as *Bruce Almighty, Liar Liar,* and *Ace Ventura, Pet Detective.* After Tom suffered a head injury, his whole life moved towards a more simplistic existence; *I Am* documented this profound journey. As I watched, I realized I had my own story that I could tell. I'd been in an accident that jolted me into a momentary freedom from my lifelong phobias, which were now seeping back into my life. Why not combine my desire to become a filmmaker with my search for why humans have seemingly irrational fears? Maybe I could interview and film different spiritual and thought leaders to find my answers.

That very same week, I was sitting at a coffee shop with my sister and happened to glance across the street. A church sign announced a speaker who would be discussing facing your fears. I really wish I could remember the exact words because I felt it was the universe calling to me to move forward with my story, and I took it as a sign that I needed to start my film project right away. I called the church to get permission to film the speaker, and off I went.

For the next five years, I built my courage muscles by reaching out to speakers, philosophers, and writers dedicated to pursuing the answers to life's mysteries. Gregg Levoy, the author of the bestseller *Callings*, allowed me to fly down to San Francisco and interview him. I filmed Ruth L. Miller, PhD, who is the editor of *The New Game of Life*, previously written by Florence Scovel Shinn. I interviewed Kris King, the founder of an organization focused on assisting people with personal health and well-being.

Through interview after interview, I learned how to set up cameras and audio equipment, and I filmed, catalogued footage, and built my editing and graphic design skills. I discovered the art of conquering light and shadows and picking the perfect backgrounds. However, every time I attempted to create a cohesive film, something went wrong, or someone helping me didn't follow through, or I lost confidence in the direction I was taking. Slowly, the project faded into the background of my chaotic life.

> *"I took the one less travelled by,*
> *And that has made all the difference."*
> **Robert Frost**

I have been on this earth for fifty-three years now. I can no longer deny that every single life event, whether I deemed it "good" or "bad," has put me on a trajectory I didn't always recognize as the path I must take.

While my documentary, which I titled *Know Fear, Know Freedom*, slipped away, the skills I learned while attempting to make it did not. I built a set of writing, marketing, and video-making skills that allowed me to create a website and launch my resume writing business. As my business grew, I contracted a videographer to help me create promotional videos for the site. During a lunch meeting, we got to talking about a psycho thriller screenplay I wrote years ago, *In Her Blood*, that was now collecting dust on a shelf. When I mentioned it had gotten attention in a few contests but nothing had ever come of it, he said, "Why don't you direct and produce the film yourself?"

I laughed at first, but those words struck a chord. I wasn't able to pull random footage together to build a case for overcoming fear; perhaps eradicating fear isn't really possible. But I *could* film people acting out a story that was already written and slap the scenes together in order, dammit!

This decision brought up a memory I had long since forgotten. When I was a kid, I was given a little 8mm camera. I spent that whole summer on my grandparents' farm pretending to be and dreaming of being a writer and filmmaker like George Lucas and Walt Disney. I wrote skits for my sister and me to perform and recorded everything around me until I ran out of film. All the puzzle pieces of my life flew into place, and I remembered what I wanted to be when I grew up!

I was still afraid, but a higher purpose overrode my fear. My writing and film endeavours, along with my communication and networking skills from my resume writing business, gave me a sense of purpose in this world, which in turn gave me the courage to keep moving forward, step by step. In spite of my palpable fear of rejection, I reached out to people to see if I could muster the resources to make my movie happen.

It took eight months to finish the film, and literally the entire city stepped up to help make this dream of mine come true. The local community college collaborated with me to contract five interns needing a project to obtain their media degrees. The City of Eugene, Oregon and the Shelton McMurphey Johnson House, a Victorian home on Skinner's Butte, loaned me the house as a set location for the whole summer. A cast of amazing people volunteered their time. Friends and family helped whenever something needed to be done. Restaurants in the area fed my crew. Every day, and with every outreached hand offering assistance, my fear and anxiety disappeared into the background, replaced by a confidence I had never felt before.

Making this movie was the hardest thing I have ever done in my life, but I wouldn't trade the experience for a million dollars. It taught me I could do anything I set my mind to. It reinforced my faith and determination to never give up. It showed me that everything that has happened in my life happened for a reason, and it has all led me to this perfect moment in time. To this day, the skills I learned through filmmaking help me with my thriving resume writing business. Being able to create and edit my own training videos for my website and blogs is a huge benefit, helping me to attract potential clients to my business every day. I can see no effort or obstacle was ever wasted.

After months of filming, re-filming, and brutal editing sessions, our feature psycho-thriller *In Her Blood* premiered at Lane Community College on November 3, 2017. Hundreds of family, friends, and community members joined us in celebrating the finished movie. Cheers erupted at the end, especially when the second surprise ending appeared on the screen. I felt like a mama bear releasing her baby into the world, and not just because of In Her Blood. Being able to work with all the young interns and actors, seeing the joy and pride in their faces at the event, and knowing they learned they could do anything if they set their mind to it was the best gift of all.

After *In Her Blood* launched on Amazon Prime, I found an old vision board I had made hidden away in my closet. My sister Brigitte and I had a tradition of taking a "sister only" trip to the coast and creating a vision board every year on January 11, her birthday, to set the tone for the rest of the year. With magazines strewn all over a hotel room, we would cut out images that spoke to us and paste them together however we felt compelled. As I examined this board, I noticed in the lower left corner a clipping of a young girl holding a boom and mic as if she was on a movie set. I didn't know what that image meant to me at the time; I just liked it and pasted it to the cardboard. But my soul knew, and it called to me. The universe, the mystic law, revealed my calling.

That tree was no accident. As cliché as it may sound, I believe that everything does happen for a reason. After that fateful day, I had a choice. I could cower in fear, allowing that smashed car to be my proof that the world was unsafe and never venture out again. Or, I could turn poison into medicine by facing my fears. I decided to take the path less travelled and created a life I could never have imagined.

About Heather Ann McBride

Heather Ann McBride is a daughter, sister, mom (of both people and cats), friend, filmmaker, upcycler, and resume writer at InClarity360. If she isn't writing a resume or on the phone with a client, she is turning junk into cool, usable things or driving to the Oregon coast to stare at the ocean. It gives her inner peace to know that she is part of something bigger in this universe. She strives to experience a human revolution each day guided by her mentor and founder of Soka Gakkai International Daisaku Ikeda, whose organization promotes a global Buddhist movement for peace, education, and cultural exchange.

www.inclarity360.com
www.inherblood.com
LinkedIn: linkedin.com/in/heathermcbride-resume-writer/

9

My Road to Self-Discovery

By Moira Ellis Lynch

"That wonderful and terribly frightening journey of self-discovery. That process of growth, of being an independent person, of learning who you are and what you want from life, is the real secret of life, happiness and beauty."
Diane von Furstenberg

My Road to Self-Discovery

By Moira Ellis Lynch

My journey of self-reflection began a number of years ago, and I have made a lot of progress in that time. However, a confrontation with a neighbour in 2019 reminded me that this journey is still ongoing. I was having some work done in my garden, and my neighbour took offense to it. He began yelling, stopping me from speaking, calling me names, and threatening me in an attempt to intimidate me. This affected me emotionally for months after, and I was disappointed that I was allowing another person to make me feel so incredibly bad about myself. I began to examine why I avoided confrontation and where my fear of disappointing people came from, and as I looked back, I could see it worked its way into my psyche at a very early age.

I'm the youngest of three children and the only girl in

my family. I was the "surprise" baby, which meant that my brothers were a bit older than me and my parents had me later in life—when I was born in the late 1960s, my mum, at the age of forty-two, was considered an "older mother." They were great people in many ways, but the generational gap between us along with the differences in their own upbringings made it difficult for us to understand each other.

My parents were very protective of me, so I lived a sheltered life as a child. I was incredibly shy and tried to always "be a good girl" and do as I was told—if I didn't, I felt incredibly guilty. As with many children who grew up around that time, any time I did something wrong I got threatened with the wooden spoon and told to "wait until my father got home." Because I was quite sensitive, I ended up being afraid of making my parents upset in any way and tried my hardest to never do anything wrong. However, I seemed to fail at this more and more as I got older and entered my teenage years—at least, that is how I perceived it at the time.

During my childhood, I was often called ugly by one person and spoiled by others, to the point that I started to believe it. Looking back now, I'm sure those people didn't intend this to be harmful—that they were just teasing or thought I was spoiled in a good way—but my sensitivity meant I believed everything anyone told me.

I was jealous of my friends with younger parents who could better relate to them and understand them. They all seemed to have happy and communicative relationships; they talked about things I wouldn't dream of talking with my own parents about. For example, I learned about the birds and the bees from a book that my mum gave me to read. I couldn't ask her anything about that subject as I was too embarrassed, and we didn't learn anything like that in school back then. The only thing she did tell me was that you do not have sex before you are married.

My brother always says that he and I had different parents, and it is true. In my mind, I saw my parents as old; his were much younger. They were far more protective of me than my brothers, and I saw this as them being controlling for a long time. Today, I believe they were just being overprotective, especially as they had dealt with hardships while they were both growing up in England during World War II. Because I was a girl, they saw me as being more vulnerable than my brothers—as is common for people of their generation—and they did what they thought they needed to do to keep me safe.

As the years passed, I started seeing how my friends were allowed to do so much more than I was, and I started resenting this. I couldn't see why I was being treated differently at the time, and this may have enhanced my sense of worthlessness.

I wanted to do the same activities as my friends, but my parents had predetermined my life for me. They enrolled me in synchronized swimming at a young age, and it became my life for a number of years. I was never asked if I wanted to swim; I was just told that I was going to do it, and I followed along so as not to disappoint them. Mum was heavily involved in fundraising for the team, and I believe she must have been quite proud of me for excelling in that sport. I just wish she had told me; instead, there was simply an expectation that my siblings and I would succeed in everything we did.

My parents also told me they wanted me to be a secretary, so most of my school subjects needed to be focused on clerical skills. In Grade Twelve, I completed my required courses to get my high school diploma in the first semester—half a year earlier than my classmates. Suddenly I had graduated high school and was working in an office while I waited to attend college in the fall. It was a lonely year. I was no longer with my friends every day, and I watched from the sidelines as they all went to graduation parties I wasn't allowed to attend. I wasn't able to participate in graduation planning during the second semester, and no one from my class contacted me to ask me to take part. My photo in the yearbook, which I had been looking forward to for so long, has nothing written about me next to my name—no nicknames and no worthy mentions. I was deflated, jealous, and felt that I missed out on so much.

Due to their protectiveness, my parents sent me out into the world unprepared for adult life. They didn't teach me important life skills such as how to save money, how to openly communicate, how to apologize, or how to admit that you've made a mistake. I believe this contributed to my lack of self-confidence and low self-esteem. Back in those teen years I had thought I was just shy, but I realize now that I was insecure and had a great amount of self-doubt. I found it terribly hard to talk to people and couldn't stand up for myself. In order to feel good about who I was, I needed to receive encouragement from the people I was always trying to please. I couldn't understand why I felt like I was constantly disappointing someone. I was conditioned to think that I should feel guilty every time I did something for myself. I didn't think I was a good person at all.

I harboured dark thoughts about my whole life purpose throughout my teenage years, and I coped by hiding my negative self-talk. I felt constricted and supressed, but because of my lack of self-confidence, I didn't know how to speak up and properly express any of this to my parents. I don't doubt their love for me at all, but I wasn't given support, encouragement, or freedom to make my own decisions or be my own person. I wasn't given solid praise to boost my self-confidence, self-esteem, or self-worth.

When I met my first boyfriend at the age of eighteen, I quickly attached myself to him for two reasons: because someone was actually paying attention to me and because I needed to escape from my parents. At age twenty, convinced it was my only option to have a life of my own, I told my parents I was moving in with my boyfriend. They didn't react well. He was six years older than me and wasn't the kind of man they wanted me to be with, so they were angry and upset. My dad even bet one hundred dollars that I would be back within six months. But the more they tried to convince me I was making a mistake, the more I wanted to prove them wrong. I just wanted to show the world that I could think for myself. I can see now how young and naïve I was and that my parents were desperately trying to protect me, but at the time I was blinded by my emotions.

My relationship with my parents was strained after I moved out, and for the first year I didn't see them much at all. However, Mum made a significant effort to try to repair things between us, especially when I needed surgery on both of my feet about three years after I left. I was unable to walk for a few weeks, and Mum supported me throughout my recovery. It was wonderful to have her help, and I am so glad that we were able to spend this time together as only two months later, she was hospitalized with pneumonia and subsequently learned she had lung cancer.

Dad took me out for my birthday dinner alone that year, and I think it was the first time I saw him as a friend. I felt bad for him as I knew he was worried about Mum, who had always been so strong and was now showing her vulnerable side.

Six weeks later, Mum was told her cancer had spread to numerous organs, including her brain. She wasn't given long to live. Thankfully, my family was able to arrange a trip to Hawaii just in time to spend her last Mother's Day in her favourite place. I was so happy to have this time with her, but there were challenging aspects to it as well. Dad was terribly stressed by the fact that Mum was so sick, and as a result he became agitated if anything went even slightly wrong. A few times, I was the one he yelled at. Mum would end up in tears, and I would feel horrifically guilty even though I knew he wasn't actually angry at me. This seemed to be a pattern in my life: other people would get angry and take it out on me, and I was so sensitive that I took everything personally and never let go of the guilt.

Mum passed away a few weeks after we returned home from Hawaii. I was relieved that she wasn't suffering anymore, but I missed her beyond belief. For years afterward, the guilt I felt for disappointing her ate away at me. I was barely able to be her friend like I was with Dad later on, and it's one of the biggest regrets of my life.

In 1996 I married my boyfriend, whom I'd now been with for ten years. I was proud to have a secure and stable career with the municipal government in the city where my parents raised me—this again was something they had wanted me to do, and I did it in hope that it would make them proud as well. I was constantly trying my best and striving to be the best I could be, always trying to prove myself. I had an extremely high work ethic and was confident while at my job, yet in my personal life I was always on guard—always fearful of making someone angry or disappointing them. I'd struggled with my self-esteem for so long that when I first heard the term self-love, I thought it was ridiculous. I had been unconsciously conditioned to think I was ugly and worthless and that there must be something wrong with me. That was my normal.

Then I joined a bowling league and met a young man who had some learning difficulties. I was shocked when, after watching me for a few weeks, he approached me and told me that I was a good person. From that day onwards, he always told me that same thing every time he saw me. After a while, I started thinking that maybe there was some truth to that. Maybe I wasn't that bad after all. My conscience fought this idea, though, and so I continued to need to prove I was good to everyone around me.

Throughout this time, I was experiencing a lot of challenges in my relationship with my husband. I overcompensated in my efforts to make him happy, but it seemed to me that the more I tried, the more I failed. I finally went so see a counsellor to discuss my struggles with feeling like I didn't exist; I was unhappy, I felt alone too often, and I felt on guard and afraid of making him angry. I stayed with him for so long because I feared no one else would ever love me, and that wasn't fair for either of us. The counsellor helped me see that I had always done everything the way everyone else wanted me to, and that I needed to have some independence and discover life on my own. So, after seventeen years together, I left and moved into an apartment in my hometown. I was in my mid-thirties and living alone for the first time, and it was the best thing I could have done for myself.

I had a lot of learning to do, and it certainly didn't happen right away. During the years that followed, I was vulnerable and got taken advantage of. I fell into the trap of being a victim and continued to overcompensate to get people's approval, to my own detriment at times. My counsellor recommended some self-help books which gave me some guidance and helped me realize that I wasn't alone in many of my issues, especially my grief for my mother. I began focusing on doing positive things for myself. And soon, I had my first "a-ha" moment: I realized that I was the one who was giving people permission to take advantage of me. I had always been so focused on the negative, and I began to wonder what my life would be like if I changed my mindset to focus on happy and fulfilling thoughts. Thus began my journey of self-discovery. There have been many ups and downs along the way, but I discover more and more about myself all the time. And over the years, I have even started to like myself. I realized that I have been a good person all along; I just couldn't always see it.

It was only after I began this journey that I was able to meet someone I could truly be happy with. In 2010, my dad and I had become great friends. He invited me to go travelling to Ireland with him that September, and I readily agreed. I was single at the time and not looking for any kind of relationship; I was enjoying life on my own. However, one of the places Dad took me was a beautiful village by the ocean, and it literally changed my life.

On the first night of our visit, we were in the pub attached to the guesthouse and, seeing as I had been singing for a few years now, I was looking forward to an evening of live music. Dad was tired so he headed off to bed, but I decided to stay up and just enjoy the atmosphere. As I walked up to the bar to get a drink, the owner asked an Irishman next to me if he could tune the house guitar. That initiated a conversation between us as I was very interested in knowing what kind of music this man played. We spent the next few hours chatting up a storm and singing a few songs with the pub patrons. He came back and met my dad the next day, and we exchanged email addresses. After six months of emails and Skype calls, we both travelled from our home countries to meet on the east coast of the USA. I was taking a huge chance by flying so far to meet up with someone I'd mostly spoken to through emails and Skype calls, but I'm so glad I did as we really hit it off.

Our long-distance relationship began, and for the next year and a half we both flew back and forth across the Atlantic every few months. My Irishman then proposed to me, and we were married in Vancouver on what would have been my parents' fifty-ninth wedding anniversary. Eight months later, we had a Celtic wedding in Ireland on the third anniversary of the day we met, held in the very place we met. It was pure magic, with family and friends from Canada, Ireland, and the UK all coming together to share this very special day with us. Our relationship is one of support and encouragement, and I'm so fortunate to have my husband with me on this continued journey. I know that if my mum were alive today, she would definitely approve.

One of the biggest breakthroughs I had, which has helped me understand why my mum was so overprotective of me, came in my mid-forties when I was told about a family secret: my mum's half-sister was actually her mother, who had her at the age of sixteen. Because of her strict upbringing, I believe Mum was fearful that I could have become a young mother myself, and in her eyes this would have ruined my life. In addition, talking to relatives about her and reading love letters between my parents that I found after my dad passed away helped me get to know the woman my mother was. I feel I know her better now than I did when she was alive.

I'm now living the life I have always wanted, and my journey continues to be one of self-discovery. I've learned that it's never too late to make amends, even if it's with yourself. I have been able to take challenging experiences, such as the experience with my neighbour, and use them to learn more about myself and further my personal growth—I was able to recognize a fear within myself and take steps to dispel it. I've had peace lately living in my home in the Welsh countryside, and I've had time to reflect and chip away at my memories. And as I do, I can see how much I've grown and discovered about who I am. I'm so grateful and proud of how much I have overcome, and I know my parents would be too.

About Moira Ellis Lynch

Born and raised in West Vancouver, Canada, Moira Ellis Lynch had a career in local government that spanned almost three decades before she relocated to the scenic countryside in rural Wales with her Irish husband. During her career, Moira worked in parks, recreation, and cultural services administration as well as human resources, holding both union and management positions.

Moira's personal interests are in the arts and include organizing special events, fundraising, singing, playing guitar, dancing, and taking part in the visual arts. She is a dedicated helper, always making someone smile with a small gesture. Her days are full of creativity—gardening, growing food, baking, gourmet cooking, painting, crafting, decorating, writing poetry, and more—as well as managing her country house and spending quality time with her husband and two cats. She and her husband enjoy travelling, entertaining, singing, and playing guitar together—and most recently, writing songs during lockdown.

Moira has had many experiences worthy of putting into a book and her plans for the future include many stories yet unwritten. She is also hoping to one day build a B&B in Ireland; in the meantime, she will just keep enjoying her happy life.

10

More Than Just a Mother

By Buffi Davids

*"Owning our story and loving ourselves through
that process is the bravest thing that we will
ever do."*
Brené Brown

More Than Just a Mother

By Buffi Davids

After becoming a mother, I felt like I had lost myself—lost my story. My children are an amazing gift, but the trade-off of my dreams and my voice was much more significant than I could have imagined. It took me a long time to learn to unapologetically step forward into a place where I could not just live as a mother, but also thrive in this role while still moving forward into my dreams. And by sharing my story, I hope I can help other women who are in the trenches of motherhood— littles swarming around them, unsure of who they presently are outside of the role of "mom"—to do the same.

When my husband and I got married, we entered this commitment with the knowledge that we most likely wouldn't have kids. We both grew up in homes with pieces of parenthood we didn't appreciate, and we didn't think we would do any better at it. So, we made the choice to break the cycle by not participating in it.

Six years into our marriage, I decided to go to baking and pastry school. I had wanted to do this right out of high school, but the cost and location were far too prohibitive back then. Now, though, I was finally in a place where this was within my reach. Now, I was living my dream. Every day I got to learn to make new things that looked and tasted incredible. The kitchens and pantries were fully stocked with ingredients I had never seen before. The options for what I could create seemed endless, and I was learning to express myself through my creations.

It was during this time that my husband and I revisited the conversation of whether or not to have kids. We had been through a lot in the last six years, including a move across the country that allowed us to live in community with my husband's family. Experiencing our three nephews was so amazing; their house always seemed to be full of excitement, adventure, and love. We decided that we would be open to having kids once I completed my schooling. However, the timing of having children does not always go to plan.

We were not yet trying, but I got pregnant partway through my course. The program was broken into three general sections followed by a specialty. While I had a relatively easy pregnancy, I chose to step away from the school at the conclusion of the last section, just before the specialty focus, as it seemed like a good breaking point for me. I figured this would be the best place for me to return to later, once my child was older and I had more space and time.

Looking back, there is a large piece of me that is thankful I stepped away when I did. My grandma became ill soon after, and because I was not working or attending school I was able to spend a lot of precious time with her before she passed. She never met my daughter, who was born three months later, but I think they are connected. I had no doubts that my baby was a girl, to the point that I never bothered to select a boy's name. My grandma and I were not always close, but we shared a birthday so we had a connection that differed from the one she shared with my siblings and cousins. I really wish she could have met my daughter, yet I feel that the time I spent with her while pregnant was a blessing to my unborn child. I named my daughter after her to honour the special connection I felt they also shared.

Being thrust into motherhood is a shock. Your days and nights become so completely taken up by this little child—people had told me this, but I didn't really understand what they meant until she was here. My ability to eat, sleep, go to the bathroom, or do anything was impacted. Then, at about nine months, she became ill and we spent a week at home. It was nothing major, just a cold, but the isolation rocked me. I entered into a brief but intense depression, and when I came out on the other side, I recognized that I needed to get out a bit more. This experience taught me that being isolated at home for an extended period of time was something I was ill equipped to handle. Some people are introverts and take joy in spending time alone; I do not.

When my daughter was four months old, I got my first glimpse of my old self. Cake decorating has always been a passion of mine, and I had wanted to start a decorating business long before I went to pastry school. Shortly before I found out I was pregnant, I received my first real order. An old friend from high school had seen the creations I made for family and friends online, and he contacted me and asked me to make his wedding cake. I was so honoured and ecstatic that I would get to use my creative ideas to put a voice to their love through the medium of cake. But now here I was, making my first paid-for wedding cake—which I also had to deliver forty-five minutes away—with my baby underfoot. She would not sleep, and it felt like she screamed the whole way through. It was definitely different than baking before I became a parent; it was so much harder. I got the cake finished on time and the bride loved it, but the experience was clouded. I had to alter several pieces from my original vision, using some pre-purchased decorations rather than making everything from scratch. My voice was visible in the decorating, but it felt muted.

I continued to make cakes for friends and family over the next couple of years, and the process got easier as my little one got older and slept more. I also took on a part-time baking job with a woman who became a treasured friend. I learned the art of making marshmallows and other amazing desserts for catered events, and I began to seriously consider starting my own cake business. However, my husband and I began talking about having another child as we both loved growing up with siblings, and soon we were pregnant once again. Remembering how hard it was to make cakes with an infant, I temporarily—or what I thought was temporarily—turned off my ovens, laid down that dream, and quieted my voice once more.

My husband is convinced that I wrestled with post-partum depression for the first two years of my son's life. He slept less than my daughter and was sick more often, creating more times of isolation. The periods of depression lasted longer and were more intense; there was a point when the depression almost won. All the pieces of me had been given over to motherhood. I had forgotten the joyful things I had once done. I had forgotten the importance of self. I took my thoughts and my dreams and shut them in a room with my cake decorating equipment to gather dust.

When my son was around sixteen months old, I almost left my family. The depression had been slowly rising, but then it struck hard. I didn't know who I was besides a mother, and I wanted to be more. I wanted to walk, no, RUN away. I wanted to leave—leave my husband, my home, my kids. And I did, in a way. When my husband came home, I would disappear. I wouldn't answer calls and would be gone until it was time for bed. Our marriage fractured. My husband didn't understand my need for space, but he gave it to me. He waited. I am thankful that I have a friend who walked this journey before me, though she chose a different path. I saw the devastation that leaving had caused in her life, so while I knew it would be a long and challenging journey, I chose to stay.

A part of me knew there was an end to this and that I would eventually find my way to the other side, even if it was the smallest part of me and even if I wasn't fully sure I would survive to find it.

I am grateful that I have another friend who allowed me to come to their home and just be. They would talk deep and they would talk light, always choosing the right one for the moment. They would listen whether I was crying softly or screaming until I was red in the face with tears streaming. They saw me. They cared for me when I didn't care for anything. They pushed me to challenge my destructive thoughts and look for life, for hope. They challenged me to find myself again.

My perception was that as a mother, I had to have it together all the time. And as a stay-at-home mom in particular, I thought I had to be with my children constantly and my house and yard had to be perfect. I felt I wasn't measuring up, and the pressure made me feel like I was drowning. When our daughter started kindergarten, my husband and I made the choice to put our two-year-old son in daycare one day a week. One day, that's all. And it was amazing. It sounds like such a small and easy thing to do, but it was difficult for me. From my space of seeing all my mom-friends who were able to do it all—who had the perfect house, perfect yard, perfect kids—I felt like I had failed. Yet I treasured this time. On that one day, I could take time to find life. To find me.

I did very little at first; mostly I walked and visited friends. But then I wanted more. Because I had slowly lost small pieces of myself over the last few years, I hadn't realized how quiet and locked away I had become. As I began to take time for myself, I realized I did not even know how much of myself I had lost. It was a revelation that I was on a journey which had just begun.

I contemplated returning to pastry school. Finishing my program would be a great step towards achieving my dream, but it was now several years since I had attended and the commute would put me away from home for almost the whole day. This was not possible for me in this season. While this should have been a bitter pill to swallow, I began to view where I was at through the lens of the journey. Flour doesn't automatically become a cake; the baker must take several things and mix them together. They have to choose whether to turn the flour into cake or bread, whether the flavour should be chocolate or vanilla. They have to mix it until every piece of each ingredient, no matter how small, is combined and covered by the others. Each choice, each change, is not the end of the journey but rather a step forward within it.

For cake to transform, it has to go through the heat and each ingredient must let go of the old to form the new. If too much salt is added or a clump of baking soda is missed in the mixing, it can mar the flavour of the entire treat. If the cake is pulled from the oven too early, it will fall to mush. If it is pulled too late, it will be burnt. Finding the right moment to take it out of the oven can be the hardest part. On my journey, I was just realizing that what I had been doing wasn't working—that I needed to find a different mix of ingredients. I had to be intentional about what I chose to bring into my recipe, though I did not yet have an idea of the timing.

A year after I began having this time to myself, I had the opportunity to volunteer in the library at my daughter's school. This restored a piece of my life! Organizing is a passion of mine and was the focus of my first career as an administrator and event planner, so going to a place where I got to organize books and complete tasks was life-giving. Children were coming and going, but they weren't my kids, nor were they my responsibility. There were also women there who became true friends as we shared our struggles and laughed together. The library was like fresh air moving through a stale building, refreshing and renewing me.

Slowly, I started to find the ingredients that were missing from the recipe of my life and regain the strength I had lost, both in body and in mind. I returned to exercise and completed three half-marathons, something that had been on my to-do list for twenty years. I also pulled some friends together and we defeated an obstacle course race, which involved twenty obstacles that push you to your mental and physical limit over twenty kilometres that ran up and down a mountain side. The pieces of myself started to fit back together again, and yet I was different. The ingredients used were the same, but what came from the oven was stronger and heartier with more depth of flavour.

The strength I gained from completing these challenges and moving forward on my journey helped push me to make another large leap. My desire for baking had not vanished, but I no longer wanted to make large cakes. Doing one would shut my house down from Wednesday to Saturday, and we'd end up ordering food and spending far too much time keeping the kids away from the sugary creations. My husband encouraged me to consider offering baked goods at the local farmers market, so I stepped in. This turned out to be another missing ingredient in my life.

I put my son in another day of daycare and began spending my Thursdays and Fridays prepping my creations for sale. I started with gourmet marshmallows, muffins, and loaves, then added hand pies to my repertoire. These pies became my main seller and a source of joy for me and my customers; they allowed me to be creative yet were still contained within a pattern. The market allowed me to use my creativity through trying new flavours, like a rich chocolate crust filled with Nutella and sweet strawberry or a buttery crust filled with peanut butter and raspberry. It also gave me a space to talk and be the extrovert that I am, and to do it with ADULTS!

I'd love to say that this is the end of my story—that I was able to find who I am and flourish. However, life has a way of continually shifting. As I was sitting in my peace, my health turned. My face and left leg started to feel numb. A few weeks later, my right hip started to ache. I didn't realize the extent of the pain until one day I had to hold the wall to stabilize myself and someone nearby asked if I needed help. I sometimes struggled to walk and could no longer run. This was a major setback, and depression reared its ugly head yet again. I was fighting my own body to even take care of my body. After a year of uncertainty, I was diagnosed with Lyme disease.

Before my health complications began, I had joined the board of the market. It was an easy commitment at first, but during the same fall as my turn in health there were a few unplanned circumstances that ended up taking more time than intended. I also missed spending Saturdays with family. So, I chose to lay down my baking to help ensure the market continued.

The spring before my son entered kindergarten, and a few months before my Lyme diagnosis, I took on a part-time administration and community building job. I saw it as an opportunity to help build my community and grow in my leadership skills, both of which are passions of mine. I was employed by a dear friend whom I had worked for years ago, and it was an honour to work with him again—until tragedy struck and he had to step away.

I stayed and spent the next year working in an ever-shifting environment with some amazing people and some toxic ones. This was a huge mistake. I had put myself out there while I was vulnerable and struggling, and I felt crushed. I stepped away just under a year later, exhausted, overwhelmed, and broken. This fed into the depression. It had me questioning my validity, my self-worth, and my ability to be anything other than "just a mom."

Three months after I stepped away from my job, before I had processed my pain from the year and the difficulty of leaving my position, the whole world changed upon the arrival of the COVID-19 pandemic. I am once again home with both of my kids as we have chosen to shift to homeschooling. I am again choosing to put myself on hold for them, and they are flourishing in this space. This choice was beneficial for them but came at a steep price for me. I have since found small activities to put them in, such as an art class, and it has slowly added up to a few hours alone throughout the week. Sometimes, that's enough. But if I am not careful, the week gets away from me and I don't have any time to return to myself.

Throughout this journey, I have come to realize that waiting until my kids are grown to take time for myself is not only bad for me, but also hurts my kids. Just like in an airplane where you put the mask on yourself before helping others, I have to be healthy myself to build a healthy space for my kids. However, it is not possible to live in a place where I am 100% okay all the time—it is an ever-changing, ever-shifting process of searching and laying down. In finding myself yet again, I am loving my husband and my kids. And in making space for myself, I am ensuring I can be there for my husband and kids when things change yet again.

Each time I find the ingredients of myself and mix them back together, the flavour is different as I am different. Each time, I have grown just a little bit.

About Buffi Davids

Buffi Davids has lived a varied life that has included careers ranging from being the production and stage manager of a symphony orchestra to the owner of a small baking company. She presently fills her days with teaching as she learns to homeschool her two active children. Her journey from the working world into motherhood and homeschooling has been an adventure that at times feels like running an obstacle course—full of difficult and unexpected challenges as well as highly fulfilling moments.

Writing has been a passion since she was a child, but for several years she had laid down her pen. It has been a joy for her to pick it up again to share a piece of her story with hopes of letting another mom know she is not alone in this ever-changing journey.

11

Finding the Lesson in the Struggle

By Tammy Haywood

"Think like a queen. A queen is not afraid to fail. Failure is another stepping-stone to greatness."
Oprah Winfrey

Finding the Lesson in the Struggle

By Tammy Haywood

The day I was declared cancer free, I felt like a fraud. It was a familiar feeling, but this time it was stronger than anything I'd experienced before. I had expected to feel elated, uplifted, like a better person, or like someone who had discovered the secret of life. Instead, I felt guilty for the attention, affection, and gifts I had received. Not only had I inconvenienced so many people over the past eighteen months, but I didn't die. I kept waiting for that "a-ha" moment, the one that everyone speaks of when they have had a similarly extreme life experience, but it never came.

My diagnosis had been earth-shattering. In 2011, we lost my father to cancer the same week as my birthday. I was heartbroken and decided that I would get a physical as a gift to my children so that we would have a healthy baseline to move forward with as I aged. I almost cancelled my mammogram—I was forty-three years old, symptom free, had no lumps, and had no family history of breast cancer. I went anyways, though, and right away I knew there was a problem. The technician kept taking images, having me wait while she went off somewhere, and then returning to take more images. I phoned my husband from my car and he reassured me that everything would be fine, but I wasn't so sure. I knew there was a bookstore across the street, so I immediately went over and found my way to the health aisle. I started desperately looking for what they may have seen and what it might mean for me.

My scan took place right before the winter holidays, so I was unable to get booked for a biopsy until the new year. The results were inconclusive. I was good to leave it at that; it had been a long year, and I was ready to move on with life. However, one of our friends is a doctor, and he urged me to move forward with a lumpectomy and a signal node biopsy.

I had my lumpectomy in March. They were unable to get clean margins—they had some of it but couldn't confirm they had all of it. Then, on April 4, I was attending a funeral when I got a call from my doctor saying that he needed to see me immediately. That was the day I learned I definitively had cancer. My husband was loving and comforted me every night as we waited with bated breath for the next step. It was hard for us to wrap our heads around how life-changing this would be.

I had heard the saying that there are families "before C" and "after C," but I hadn't fully understood what it meant until it happened to me. There is no other way I can explain the experience other than that it was surreal. One day everything is life as usual, and then suddenly you are given a frightening diagnosis and every waking moment is filled with fleeting thoughts of "what if."

Because my husband had lost his own mother to cancer when he was a child, I opted for a double mastectomy—I had heard of cancer coming back years later and could not imagine my family going through that worry twice. I was decisive in a way I could never have imagined before this happened. My family is part of a tight-knit community, and because of this my husband and I opted to tell our children the full extent of my diagnosis. We were afraid they may overhear someone speaking about it and be worried or unwilling to voice their own fears.

I had a couple of amazing experiences prior to my surgery, and one in particular lifted me in a way I could never have imagined. A mother from my children's school approached me and asked if she could host a tea party for me. She asked for a guest list and then instructed everyone to bring meals to alleviate the pressures of cooking while I was recovering. I was surprised at the generosity of the women who attended, but most of all, I was surprised by the love that I felt.

My surgery was on a Monday in June, and by Friday I was ready to get dressed, put on my makeup, and accompany my husband to school to pick up our children. I was tired, but it was a priority for me. These moms had supported me, and I needed them to see I was okay. I also felt compelled to show them that if any of them had to go through something like this, they would be okay as well.

I was working as a freelance interior designer, and while I had worked professionally in the field in my early twenties, I had been off for a long time to raise my children. Without a clear plan to return to work, I had begun working on design projects for friends and gradually expanded my clientele. I had built a portfolio and now had a small, stable set of regular clients who kept me busy and referred me to their contacts.

These referrals were a mixed blessing. I was always excited for the work, but I was also faced with crippling anxiety throughout each project. Because anxiety is so prevalent in our society, I initially brushed it off as a career hazard. In truth, though, what I was experiencing was a case of impostor syndrome.

Impostor syndrome is defined as a persistent feeling that everything you have achieved came from luck and not merit. There are five types of people who are likely to experience this anxiety—experts, perfectionists, natural geniuses, soloists, and superheroes—and I can identify with all of them in some way. I feel a need to know everything before I start anything. I see the things I could have done better and not the things I have done well. As a child, I rarely had to work for good grades. I tend to believe I can do things best by myself and therefore have been denied many opportunities for mentorship. And when I am on a project, I become obsessed at the expense of my health and my time with family.

While I didn't recognize it at the time, my feelings of fraud as a cancer survivor also came from this long-cycled loop playing in my brain. It came from things like having a brother who was only months younger than me but excelled athletically—something that was very important in my family—whereas I did not. It came from growing up with parents who would ask what happened to any marks I missed before celebrating the marks I achieved. It came from being incredibly detail-oriented and feeling like every extra minute could be used to make something just a little bit better, even when I had run out of minutes. I am in no way blaming anyone for the anxiety I felt; I am just recognizing experiences that may have led to unhealthy thought patterns and perhaps helping others recognize the same. It is only through awareness that we can move on to healing.

My experience with cancer did not give me that magical moment of clarity. Instead, it led me to a path that would help me find and practice skills that have given me a sense of self-worth I may never have otherwise experienced. I think it was a catalyst for me to be able to recognize and admit that my life wasn't perfect—it wasn't an immediate realization, but it was a significant one. I had been hiding my own vulnerability for my entire life, as have many other women I have met, and then the cancer diagnosis and treatment put it on display for all to see. People were receptive to my situation, and in their kindness, they treated me as though I had been heroic in some way. This was humbling, and it fuelled my desire for personal growth as I yearned to be deserving of this attention.

One of the first steps I took to help myself feel worthy of my successes was to strengthen my career confidence. Most of my work experience has been either in family business or self-employment, so I have always questioned my ability to gain traditional employment if and when I needed to. I expressed my interest in getting a job to my family, and soon my adult son called to tell me about a position in his company that he thought would be a good fit: a conference producer for medical events. I had the university degree they wanted, but I had zero experience. My son convinced me that I would be up to the job—that I was organized, loved to research, and was interested in health.

My son was right, I loved working on these conferences. The only challenge was that I wanted more hours to get everything done. I would be up in the middle of the night calling people in every time zone. I would stop to make dinner and then go back to work as soon as it was done. There was always something I could do to make it just a little better, and I was determined to show my colleagues that I was worth the gamble. When my three-month contract expired, I had fully produced three conferences and had the beautiful, shiny brochures to show for it. I was offered a full-time contract, but I passed as the long hours were hard on my family. However, this was a very important exercise for me because I found comfort in knowing I was actually employable and had been visibly successful in this position.

Throughout this time, I continued running my own design business, which is my passion. I love the people I work with, and the flexibility is more conducive to my family's lifestyle. After I turned down the conference producer contract, a couple of clients I had done some single-family homes for asked me to become involved in a multi-family complex. I was honoured, but I wasn't sure I was ready for a project like this—it had a larger schedule, a more stringent timeline, and a strict budget. My old loop started playing. What if I couldn't do this? What if these people, who thought I was good at design, found out I was in over my head?

In the end, they convinced me that I could do it, and I suddenly moved from residential property into investment property. This project was the first successful venture in a line of projects we completed together, and I will always be grateful for the belief that these people had in me and their ability to push me to take the next step in my business.

Being afraid of risk and new challenges means that there are opportunities I have missed and doors I have never opened. For me, the idea of failure is overwhelmingly paralyzing. If I can't be the best at something, I don't want to do it. I shudder at the idea of repeating anything over and over—having never been involved in sports, I was never aware of the importance of practice. I have since sought out situations that make practice necessary in order to force myself to get past this desire for instant perfection. I still feel angst, but every exposure helps to make me more comfortable and I have grown to accept that I am a work in progress.

One of the things that has encouraged me to allow myself to be challenged is the awareness that my daughter is watching me. How can I expect her to be brave and love herself if I am not the one to teach her? I love all my children, but when my daughter was born I identified with the fact that, as a woman, I could be her most significant role model. When I see her, I sometimes see the little girl that I once was. When I think of the things I have said to myself, I shudder to think of anyone speaking those words to her. The empathy I feel for her has extended to my younger self; I now experience a sense of sadness, forgiveness, understanding, and love for who I have been and who I am becoming.

My fiftieth birthday came out of nowhere. I was working on some display suites that needed to be ready for the upcoming weekend, so when the kids called to see about dinner I had to pass. It was not the birthday I had anticipated, but I was doing something I loved for people who trusted me and I needed to get it done before I could enjoy any festivities.

My celebration happened a few days later. A girlfriend had booked tickets to a charity event that weekend and a limo to get there, and she invited my husband and me, along with some mutual friends, to join her and her husband. I decided to wear a shorty romper to this event, and while that may seem insignificant, it was a huge deal for me. I have always been body dysmorphic and hated the idea of showing my legs. However, I had recently been working with a trainer and not only did I feel great, but for the first time in years I actually believed that I looked great. I was photographed at the event, and although it may sound crazy, I congratulated myself for being able to later share that photograph. I was proud of my appearance and felt good in my skin. I had come a long way.

It had been a year of professional success for me. I had wrapped up my most expensive single-family home ever and had done multiple multi-family projects. However, I was starting to feel stagnant. I loved my work, but it was largely done in isolation. I missed the synergy of learning with others.

Then, opportunity arose; my friend who had salvaged my birthday invited me to join her in a business venture. It was for a company that used network marketing, which is a largely misunderstood platform that can be threatening to people who have either had bad experiences themselves or know someone who did. This is unfortunate because it is a career that levels the playing field for people who do not have formal education—anyone and everyone has the same potential for unlimited income. It is also an opportunity to own your own business with limited investment. There is training, support, and people within your organization who will push you out of your comfort zone and help you succeed.

In the past, my need to master this new experience would have had me retract, wait, research, and eventually miss the opportunity all together. This time, though, I realized that the launch and educational event in Louisville wouldn't wait. I thought to myself, what kind of example would I be setting for my children if I missed out on doing something that excites me? So, rather than pulling back, I dove in. Wanting to fully understand the business opportunity my friend was offering, I flew with her to the event and fell in love with the product. I was impressed by the research and could see huge potential for the technology, and I returned home excited to share the information I had gained.

Not long after, I was out walking with a friend—someone

who is also fully successful in her own business—and started to tell her about what I was doing. I was excited and full of enthusiasm for my new project. I explained how I saw an opportunity to learn many new skills, meet new people, and be able to achieve financial success through another vehicle. I could not have been more surprised when this friend decided to join me. She also has a daughter and, along with being interested in the product, she could appreciate the opportunity to acquire skills that would be useful for her other businesses. We both relished the chance to show our daughters that as women in our fifties, we were still ready to seize the day, learn new things, and be challenged.

For over a year now, I have been blessed by this community. I have especially appreciated the opportunity to acquire and try out new skills, such as social media, which I can also apply to my design business. Sometimes you have to learn by fire, and this network marketing position certainly forced me to apply social media in ways I never would have considered before. I have also found that upping and expanding my skillset is helping me cope with those crippling moments when I am afraid I am going to be called out—the more I know, the less I doubt myself in all aspects of my life. My friend and I continue to run our businesses, but this new venture has been an opportunity for us to challenge ourselves so we can grow and develop skills and confidence that otherwise may not have been accessible to us.

Through everything that has happened, I have learned that there is little that matters outside of your own experience. When I leave this earth, I want my children to know that I have grown into my potential, and I do this by trying to give myself chances to fail at something new. Without failure, there is little opportunity to learn and succeed. Success does not have to be big—it can be posting a story in a new app, finishing off a large design project, teaching your child to walk, or simply holding your partner's hand. What's important is that you do something that matters to you and to the people you love.

I have heard people say that their cancer diagnosis was a gift, but that wasn't my experience. Instead, it was the journey that came afterward that taught me so much about myself. Prior to my surgery, my value was strongly correlated in my own mind with my physical state. Parting with my breasts did not come easily to me—it challenged my body image and my sexuality, and it made me fearful that I would be less desirable and unlovable. I now recognize my own bravery and how my personal growth has helped me to feel better in my own skin than ever before. I am proud to be a role model for my children, especially my daughter, and to see how the actions I take impact them as well. I discovered that my feelings of being a fraud are completely unfounded, and that I am deserving of every accolade I have received. I have opened myself to new opportunities, which have brought me joy and fulfillment

I am grateful for the love of my family and friends, and I am learning to celebrate myself. Little by little, I am ridding myself of that little voice in my head that says I only got to where I am because I am lucky, that I don't have the skills, that I haven't earned it. I am learning to experience daily failures along with the successes, and I am learning to forgive myself when I struggle—because sometimes, the lesson is in the struggle.

About Tammy Haywood

Tammy is a serial entrepreneur who learned at her father's feet, so it's no surprise that her husband and two grown sons all run their own separate businesses. She is a firm believer in the motto, "Do what you love and the money will follow."

Tammy's sensitivity to ambiance and beautiful spaces led her into the field of interior design, where she has achieved success as a freelance designer with projects ranging geographically from Florida to Whistler in addition to building her dream home in Pitt Meadows. Tammy achieved her Bachelor of Arts at the University of British Columbia with a major in psychology.

Raised in West Vancouver, she has a love of the mountains and the ocean and continues to enjoy connection to lifelong friends. She has three children, including a daughter who has inspired her to become the best female role model she can be. As a news junkie and voracious reader, Tammy excels at research and writing and is interested in travel, culture, and current events. She shares a passion for health and wellness with her current business partners.

Email: tammy@smartypants.ca
Instagram: @mzz_smartypants
Instagram: @styliciousdesign
Facebook: Tammy Haywood

Kelly Snider
Founder of Epic Exchanges

Kelly has been a storyteller, a dreamer and a connector of people for over twenty years. As an event producer, she crafted each event to highlight her client's individual stories and needs. Since the 1990s, Kelly's story-focused events have raised over twelve million dollars net for North American charities.

Kelly's mission has always been to inspire others through sharing the stories that connect us all. She has utilized her events, the Power of Story Conference in 2017, the podcast Epic Exchanges, and now the Epic Exchanges book series, to help others find the gifts in their stories in order to share, inspire, and transform lives. Kelly excels in finding the things that connect people; whether it is charity, food and wine, or just good conversation, she is able to see the possibilities that are often overlooked in both business and personal interactions. Kelly's generosity in sharing her own stories has emboldened many to find the freedom and the strength to share the own stories.

The Back Story

I never really thought my story was anything special and

certainly not that it could help anyone. In fact, my story made me feel like a victim: someone to be pitied, someone weak.

When I was three years old, my parents fell asleep while smoking and started a house fire that took their lives. I was rescued by a good Samaritan who was passing by driving his daughter to work in the early hours of the morning. And my sister, eighteen months old at the time, was rescued by the firefighters who arrived on scene a few minutes later.

We were fortunate. We had grandparents who took us in for several weeks before my godparents legally added us to their family. We grew up with two other siblings, four sets of grandparents, and four families' worth of aunts and uncles and cousins, and we never wanted for anything. And yet, that label of orphan or adopted always made me feel less-than in some way. I felt I had something to prove: my worth, my value, my strength.

Upon my grandfather's death, we were cleaning out his apartment and I discovered a file full of newspaper clippings and other documents surrounding the fire. I learned more about the man who rescued me and found out that he'd been a teacher in the neighbouring school district. There were photos of him and his daughter, a follow-up article about him receiving a medal of bravery, and a copy of the letter from my grandfather nominating him for this very medal.

I wanted to find this man even though I estimated him to be in his eighties by this point. I tried the school district offices. I tried asking some of the educators I knew. I got nowhere.

Then I thought perhaps I could find him through his daughter. But of course, I didn't know where she might be or if she'd married or anything else. So I posted the newspaper articles on Facebook in a group dedicated to my city. I thought that there would be someone in this group who possibly had worked with her or gone to school with her who might speak up and help me get in contact.

Unbelievably, the very first comment on that post was from a woman who said, "That's me!" Then she said, "Were you the little girl?"

But that wasn't all that happened. The post started getting more and more comments: neighbours who remembered my parents and the tragedy, a firefighter who worked the scene who then gave up the profession because it hit so close to home for him and his family, the police officer who had been in his first week on the job and had to make the notification to my grandparents that their daughter and son-in-law had just passed away, and even people who had lived in the same home before and after that event.

I started receiving emails and text messages from friends who had spent the morning in tears seeing it all unfold—and some wondering why they didn't know this part of my story before now. There were so many people coming together to share their experiences and feelings around this one moment in time; a moment that was more than thirty years in the past.

This was when I started to realize that my story wasn't about weakness and wasn't something that would bring pity, but rather it was about strength—the strength to overcome and to rise up above any form of challenge. And not only do I have a story, but everyone has a story that points to their strength.

When we start to share our stories—the good and the bad, the traumatic and the triumphant—we inspire others. We encourage them to make it through their own difficult times and to keep pursuing their dreams.

Your story is a gift. And OUR stories are the gifts we can give to others.

Epic Exchanges Media

Do you have a story that you're ready to share? You could be one of the featured authors in our next book, scheduled to debut in September 2021. Connect with us!

Epic Exchanges the Podcast: Apple Podcasts and YouTube
Website: www.epicexchanges.com
Instagram: @epicexchanges
Facebook: www.facebook.com/EpicExchanges
Email: info@epicexchanges.com

Made in the USA
Coppell, TX
25 February 2021